"*Elmer Towns' book presents a clear picture of what is happening in the world of education today. The American public, including many Bible-believing Christians, have long resisted the reality of the situation. Dr. Towns' book brings into clear focus the mushrooming problems of secular education and the resulting boom in conservative Protestant Christian schools. It is clearly time for the American public in general and the Christian community in particular to come to its senses, declare an educational emergency, and support an educational program that will not kick the spiritual stuffings out of the next generation!*"

—DR. PAUL A. KIENEL, Executive Director, California Association of Christian Schools

Have the

Public Schools

"Had It"?

HAVE THE PUBLIC SCHOOLS "HAD IT"?

Elmer L. Towns

publishers since 1798

THOMAS NELSON INC.

NASHVILLE / NEW YORK

Copyright © 1974 by Elmer L. Towns
All rights reserved under International
and Pan-American Conventions
Published by Thomas Nelson, Inc., Nashville, Tennessee
Library of Congress Cataloging in Publication Data

Library of Congress Cataloging in Publication Data

Towns, Elmer L
  Have the public schools "had it"?

  Includes bibliographical references.
  1. Public schools—United States. I. Title.
LA217.T68   371'.01'0973   74–4086

Dedicated to my public school teachers who were to me what they should have been

Romana Riley
Grace Cubbage
Victoria Kennickel
Margaret LaFar
Margaret Logan
Charles J. DeMars
William B. Lain

Contents

Preface

The average visitor to a public school is immersed into a totally new experience, much different from what he expected to find. The public school is vastly changed from the one he attended years ago. Multimillion dollar buildings are shining examples of modern technology, but the facilities seem sloppier: paper in the hall, panes of glass knocked out, water coolers inoperative, lockers and walls sprayed with paint, and general rowdiness in behavior that borders on silent defiance.

Kids scuff down the hall in draggy jeans, bare midriffs, and hot pants. The middle-class parent may be shocked to see bra-less girls or boys in tank shirts. Even bare feet are not uncommon in warm climates.

But the student's attitude has always been more significant than his dress. Just as outward decorum reflects inner character, sloppy dress betrays insolence. It's not the students' "Yeah." It's not their defiant gaze. It's not their silent rage. It's not their refusal to answer questions; it's the verbal abuse that teachers have to take. Teachers are cursed . . . yelled at . . . threatened . . . slapped . . . knifed . . . and raped. Those who think that student anarchy reigns only in inner-city schools are sadly mistaken; rebellion is evident in the lily-white suburbs.

But what students don't do is just as critical as their destructive attitudes. It's obvious that students don't pray or read the Bible. These religious functions have been ruled out by the Supreme Court. In some schools the pledge to the flag is missing. Administrators have found it is easier not to "hassle" when the minority raises an objection. Other administrators mistakenly think it's wrong to force students to perform an act of public declaration of allegiance when pupils lack sincerity in their gestures.

Students don't stay in school all day. They are given permission to leave when they don't have classes. Students are not taught reverence for institutions, are not encouraged to be clean in hygiene and habit, and are not punished for breaking rules. Students are not generally appreciative of the multi-million dollar educational facilities including teaching aids, learning enrichment labs, sport facilities, libraries, and countless other educational advantages generally unheard of 50 years ago.

What in the name of outrage is going on!!

The public school is in trouble. This book examines the extent of the damage. It asks the question "Have the public schools 'had it'?" I have not attempted to answer the question. Rather, the evidence is presented. Like the jury, you must make your own decision.

I have purposely avoided quoting some of the literature that currently attacks the public school. Some of
these criticisms are emotional, others are prejudiced. My
quotations come, in the main, from the educational community. These "responsible" evaluations of public school
weaknesses cannot be ignored.

This volume does not accept the "conspiracy theory" as
the major problem of the public schools. Some organizations attempt to blame the problems of our schools on
Communist infiltration. I'm sure it has had some adverse
influence on our educational procedure, but the major
problem with public schools is Americans, not Communist. We are squatting in the hole we've dug.

The major problem of the public school is moral. As
educators have extracted religious indoctrination from
classrooms, they have also removed the American ethic
which is based on Christianity. (But, this volume does not
advocate making Christian schools out of public schools.
See Chapters eight and nine.)

I have spoken in 74 of the 100 largest churches in
America (*Christian Life* Magazine, October, 1973). In
addition, I've visited many other churches, writing stories
for *The Sword Of The Lord, The Christian Bookseller*
and *Christian Youth Today,* magazines where I regularly
publish. In these churches, I observed an abundance of
Christian schools. The impression slowly deepened that
the movement was much larger than anyone realized.
Then I examined small churches and found them in the
business of weekday Christian education. Out of my concern for Christian education in the church, my concern
for weekday Christian education intensified. Was this an
instrument to be used by God in our nation? If God was

going to use it, I wanted to know where, how, and to what extent.

I believe in private school education. My oldest daughter graduated from Lynchburg (Virginia) Christian Academy, and my other two teen-agers now attend Bible Baptist Day School in Savannah, Georgia.

May this book accomplish the aims that have been invested by many.

ELMER L. TOWNS
Savannah, Georgia

1 The Smell Of Deterioration

Some educators are nervously whispering in private what was never discussed 20 years ago—specifically, that public education has "had it." R. W. Seltzer has done more than privately talk about it; he published an article titled, "Public Education, Is Its Demise Near?" in *The Clearing House* magazine: "At the present rate of deterioration, public education as it exists today will be dead and buried by the year 2000." [1] Liberal columnist Stewart Alsop agrees, noting, "Public education is in danger of collapse," and "the trouble goes far beyond the school's all-too-frequent failure to teach Johnny to read. A terrifying increase in hard drug use and equally terrifying increase in violence in our schools are now the principle threat."

William Waugh, the Associated Press education writer, puts it: "America's high schools—from the ghetto to the suburbs—are like boiling cauldrons.[2] No one can predict when the pot will boil over, but already violence, vandalism and noisy protests are common." According to Waugh, "Students from New York to California say their schools operate in a prison-like atmosphere—armed guards, fenced school yards, and . . . locked classroom doors."

Lee Dolson, President of the San Francisco Classroom

Teachers Association, demanded an end to school violence, maintaining, "Teachers are in a constant state of fear." His teachers face mockery, threats, and verbal abuse that shouldn't be permitted in a society of decent people. They want a reversal of trends to lawlessness, "even if it takes police patrolling the halls of every school." *U. S. News & World Report* cites teacher frustration after a meeting with the Board of Education, because news of attacks upon teachers is kept out of newspapers by the Board, in an effort to prevent other attacks. One questions if a "conspiracy of silence" does not reward the unpunished and unknown attacker. Under the cloak of anonymity, he is motivated to further acts of violence. The magazine notes:

With the increase in crime and violence in public schools, many principals are reportedly preoccupied now with "hushing up" cases of violence in their schools—even though hiding the facts encourages further misbehavior.

Dolson observes the increase in absenteeism among teachers who phone in ill, because they are too sick (from fear) to go to school.

The American public has paid through the nose to provide the best educational facilities ever. Yet they are now paying well over $200 million per year for school vandalism. A school maintenance man of foreign descent in New York City pointed to an empty frame where glass had been broken: "That's the third time this year I have put glass in that spot." He pointed out that children in his home country respected their teachers and took care of their buildings. Some architects are advising windowless schools to alleviate the high cost of glass breakage. If the American society no longer respects the educational process, how can we expect the children to have a higher regard for school? As a result, students vent their wrath on school buildings; so much so that night lights, chain-link fences, night watchmen, dog guards, alarm systems, or some other available created preventative device is purchased with tax money to protect the money already invested in schools.

"The cities have been murdered by their schools," said Jerrold R. Zacharies, Professor of Physics at the Massachusetts Institute of Technology and a leading pioneer in recent education innovation. "If the schools were good, we could handle the other problems." [3] Writing in the *National Observer,* Jerrold Foutlick states, "New York City spends twice as much on education as it did six years ago and the percentage of children below minimum comprehension in reading has increased."

An older adult would be shocked if he walked the halls of a typical 1974 high school (if he could gain entrance without an ID card or special permit). The halls are strewn with litter, paper, cans, and trash. In the rest rooms there is an unbearable odor of urine, defecation, and smoke. Bronze handles on water fountains are hammered into uselessness. Windows are broken, grass and shrubbery are ravished. In 1972, New York schools suffered $2 million in window breakage alone, and 196 schools reported a fire. Los Angeles taxpayers had to cough up $1.9 million for vandalism. A white collar community, Elk Grove, Illinois, a suburb of Chicago, spent $20,000 for stolen equipment and breakage.

Some feel public schools are already dead. At least they would bury the concept of community schools. A funeral was held in the Spring of 1973 sponsored by "Citizens for Community Schools," a 14,000-member parent organization that protested busing children criss-cross Prince George's county in Maryland. The 83-car processional wound its way over county roads following a pickup truck with a black box symbolically containing the corpse of neighborhood schools. TV cameras and newspaper men reported the interment, presided over by a clergyman and witnessed by lawmakers and parents, black and white alike protesting busing. Recently a parent in the county complained, "I get mad seeing my kid bused 22 miles, and I can't get gas to drive to work."

Only the charred walls were left standing when a $1.5 million fire destroyed the Washington Junior High School at Joliet, Illinois, in 1967; three separate fires were set before 6:00 a.m. The J. D. Dickerson Elementary School in Vidalia, Georgia, was hit by arson fires on December 23, 1973, causing an estimated $100,000 damage. Between these two blazes, millions of dollars in buildings and equipment have been gutted by fire.

There is growing rebellion in the school system, as reflected by the *New York Times* during the spring of 1969. The following news reports come from the public schools of New York.

The most readily accessible instruments of rebellion are the fire alarms. They are now sounded two or three times a day, according to Max Epstein, an assistant principal (at Sands Junior High School in Brooklyn) . . . Vandalism, too, plagues the school. So many windows have been broken lately that the empty panes are being filled with nonbreakable transparent plastic. So much clothing has been stolen from the coatrooms that many students carry their coats with them through the day . . .

Weekend burglaries have become so common—including a series of thefts in which all 33 typewriters from the typing classroom disappeared—that an expensive alert system is being installed that automatically telephones the police precinct and plays a recorded call for assistance . . . (*New York Times*, February 23, 1969).

The problems of pupils within the public schools seem to intensify when they strike out against lawlessness and let their voice be heard. One pupil who attempted to do something about the problem of violence suffered the following:

Detectives of the Liberty Avenue station in Brooklyn said yesterday that they were investigating the stabbing Saturday night of a white student who attends Thomas Jefferson High School. The police said the student, Leo Andreoli, had been attacked 16 blocks from the school by three Negro youths whom he said he did not know.

Young Andreoli has emerged as a spokesman for a group of white students who attend the racially troubled predominantly Negro high school at Pennsylvania and Dumont Avenues, in the East New York section. Last week he was part of a contingent of white students who went to City Hall to protest alleged racial slurs by Negro students during a school assembly program (The *New York Times*, February 21, 1969).

But no one should be misled to think that the malignancy in public schools is caused simply by a small criminal gang. The cancer that grows in our school system may be in its terminal stages. Many students are infected, and their mass hysteria sometimes leads to mob action.

Eastern District High School in Brooklyn, where about 200 students broke glass partitions and windows and threw furniture about on Friday, will be closed to students tomorrow for cleaning and repairs. About $4,500 worth of damage was caused by the rampage in the school . . . (The *New York Times*, March 9, 1969).

Five days later the *Times* carried this report of yet another incident:

About 900 students were forced to leave classes at Central Commercial High School in midtown Manhattan yesterday after a gas bomb was set off on the fourth floor. An official there said the incident was "isolated" from disorders at other schools.

Our students have been told to express themselves—they do. Our students have been told to demand their rights—they do. Our students have been told to defy injustice—they do. But their self-expression is outside the law. Their demands are without a rational basis. Their defiance of injustice is aimed at the wrong cause, because that which they defy is not injustice, but their personal prejudice.

Student demonstrations and disruptions plagued several city high schools yesterday, forcing the closing in midafternoon of two schools in Brooklyn. Minor fires broke out at two schools, causing slight damage but no injuries.

One fire started in the gymnasium of Erasmus Hall High School shortly after 22 youths were arrested during demonstrations outside the building . . . Another fire in a basement supply closet, forced the evacuation of DeWitt Clinton High School in the Bronx. Classes were resumed later, but many students stayed out, joining a protest that was under way outside the building.

Yesterday had been designated as "D-Day" by a coalition of Negro and Puerto Rican high school students who recently submitted a list of 15 demands to city school authorities . . . Among the demands listed in the publication were "no more suspensions" of students, "no cops in schools," "no program cards" for students (the "teachers have no right to tell us where we can or cannot go in the schools") and "an end to general and commercial diplomas" (The *New York Times*, April 22, 1969).

These few insights into our schools sound like the introductory scenes of a horror movie where someone is massacred in every other scene. The story gets more gory before it's over. The case against the public school reeks like their dirty rest rooms. Some literature books read like the bathroom walls. Young "latrine lawyers" sneer at educators. "You can't touch me," they say, and defy discipline.

High school seniors are not scoring as well on the two major college admission and placement tests in 1972-73 as they did a decade ago, according to results released by the College Entrance Examination Board and the American College Testing Program.[4] The median score in verbal ability fell from 478 to 445 during the last ten years on the scholastic aptitude test of the college boards taken annually by over a million high school students. Even though educators are given the "trust" of the young and are "charged" to provide them with an education, they have come up with three excuses for the dip in scores. First, educators claim the curriculum has changed in the past decade to include more nontraditional courses. Dr. Lee Munday, ACT Vice-President for Research, said, "Ten years ago 90 percent of the kids in the eleventh grade studied American literature. That's less true today." The second reason for the low score is that a larger number of those tested include minority or low-income students. Historically, they do not do as well on standardized tests as middle-class whites. A third reason was given by Dr. T. Anne Cleary, of the College Board, who cited the negative influence of television on the reading ability of American youth. These excuses for low scores are an indictment against the educational system. Why did the system delete traditional academic courses? It has had minority and low-income students for twelve years of their life. Why has it not done a better job?

Many educators agree that the public school is in trouble, but only a few prophets predict the demise of the vast educational school system, one of the largest and most expensive educational enterprises conceived by man. When this volume asks, *"Have the public schools 'had it'?"* a question of such staggering proportion needs analysis. America is changing. The turmoil of flux is reflected in her schools. Whether or not the schools have *caused* our problems will be examined later. Some defenders of the public schools claim that schools only mirror the evolution of society.

Surely a system absorbing the energies of 62.8 million people in the United States, spending $90 billion this year, could never collapse—could it? A total of 59.5 million students are enrolled in our schools, being taught by three million teachers, supervised by 300,000 superintendents and principals. Can an industry that absorbs three out of every ten American people fade out of existence? The total expenditures for education during 1971 amounted to eight percent of the gross national product (GNP). Our schools are among the largest landowners in the nation. The teachers belong to one of the largest unions in America. Surely they would do all within their power to protect their livelihood! No one has estimated the amount of the GNP spent by the countless businesses supporting public schools—such as educational equipment, books, clothes, buses, and shoes. Could we in our wildest imagination conceive of the insurmountable problems of liquidating the multi-billion dollars in physical assets of buildings and equipment that have been purchased with taxpayers' money over the years? How could anyone suggest the collapse of such an enormous complex as the public school system, the greatest contributor to American free enterprise?

Those who suggest the passing of the school system are actually predicting the collapse of the entire American way of life, because tentacles from the school reach into every family, affecting business, clubs, church, and manufacturing plants in the nation. If the school goes, the nation—like the captain of the ship—goes down with her. Our schools are not merely a *product* of America, nor are they simply the *cause* of our nation; our classrooms *are* the United States. Because the activity in our schools, like the child in the womb, both *are* life and determine its extension.

To ask, "*Have the public schools 'had it'?*" is not suggesting schools will go out of existence. This is unthinkable. Too many people have invested too much money, accomplishing too much good. But the schools as we have known them have "had it." They have emerged with a different purpose, taking on a new complexion than in the past.

What has "had it" in public schools? Bible-reading and prayers are not legal; they have "had it." The Puritan/Protestant ethic as a style of life has been edged out by the new morality; it has "had it." Dedication to academic pursuits is no longer prized by the majority of educators; it has "had it." Correct behavior, according to respected society norms, is no longer enforced; it has "had it." Since our schools have changed, our nation will be different. This book asks the question, "*Have the public schools 'had it'?*" but the question that screams for answer is, "*Has our nation 'had it'?*"

Every social grouping of people emerges out of an historical need, intermeshes according to mutual expectation, and remains cohesive in the face of threat because of a commonly shared goal. Can the new society that is propagated by our schools successfully replace the working agreement that has built the United States? The public school does not put the same emphasis on past history that it once did. There is a new ethic by which society relates. Can the subconscious understanding hold our nation together? If it can't, the public schools are responsible, for they have either propagated a new but inoperative morality, or they haven't been faithful in their trust of communicating the past agreement that has been society's underpinnings.

Many elusive educators are supradefensive of the public school. When failures of society are nailed to their doors, they are quick to claim the school only mirrors society, and school problems only reflect cultural problems. On the other hand, public schools are accused of ignoring the past—with its commitment to God-consciousness, personal discipline, free enterprise, morality, and scholarly pursuits. Quickly the defenders reply that the schools must be relevant and meet the challenge of the future. Appealing to circular arguments, the public school educators are slow to assume any responsibility for the present evils of society. They are equally slow to take responsibility for the failures within the public schools. If the failures of society are not theirs, if the failures within their buildings are not theirs, who can we blame? They are responsible for what goes on in our schools, and the schools are given the task of perpetuating our society according to the Constitution. The pathetic arguments of educators are heard, "How can we have a disciplined school when our nation is so disrupted?" The answer is obvious: Educators have simply failed the trust that has been given them.

Taxpayers are nauseated by the stench and refuse to

approve more taxes. Drug pushers invade the scene because the public doesn't seem to care; the administrators are handcuffed, and kids are an easy prey. Unionism spreads through the teacher ranks because their jobs are threatened. Forced busing creates more permanent scars than the intended therapy. Bureaucratic inertia paralyzes the system. Kids score lower on standardized tests. Cleanliness, decency, and courtesy are discarded as the useless running board on a car.

Therefore we ask the obvious question, *"Have the public schools 'had it'?"*

NOTES

1. R. W. Seltzer, "Public Education, Is its Demise Near?" *The Clearing House*, (Vol. 1, No. 1.), p. 6-9. There are many articles and books criticizing the public schools arising outside of the educational community. Some of these are emotional, others speak from a bias. The author has attempted to use sources that would be respected by the educational community. Then opinion makers (i.e. media, legislators, educators, etc.) might re-evaluate the trends of public schools.

2. The following quotations of public school educators were taken from Gary Allen, *Public Schools They're Destroying Our Children* pamphlet available from *American Opinion*. Belmont, Massachusetts, p. 1-2.

3. As quoted by Jerrold K. Foutlick, *The National Observer*, September 1, 1969, p. 18.

4. The results of the testing were summarized in an article by Bart Barnes, "Two Testing Agencies Say Scores Falling in College Entrance," *The Washington Post*, Sunday, December 23, 1973, p. A8.

2 How Bad Are
The Public Schools?

A college professor with stomach cramps was rushed to the hospital. After a battery of tests, the doctors found nothing, so he remained under the care of nurses for several days and returned home when he began feeling better. Within thirty days, the cramps reappeared. This time his wife also was afflicted. Her cramps were worse and her vision blurred. The couple were rushed to the hospital. After nine days of diagnostic tests, again the doctors found nothing. In three weeks, the couple, along with their little boy, were readmitted to the hospital. This time the father was on the verge of death. The doctors were perplexed. After exhausting every known test, they couldn't find the source of the problem. Through a quirk of circumstances, a friend discovered he was being poisoned by lead. The couple, along with that friend, had bought some painted pottery in Mexico. The lead base paint had not been completely covered by the sealer in the baking process. The family was poisoning itself with hot chocolate served from the lead-painted pottery.

Are the Causes Known?

The American public schools are in trouble, and one authority after another has attempted to diagnose this problem, yet the causes are so *indiscernable* that the problems of our schools are missed by the average observer.

An extremely powerful poison was used in an attempt to clear a London slum of rats. Corn kernels were dipped in the poison and set out for the rats. Upon their first taste, the rodents promptly dropped over dead, yet the poison was ineffective. After the first rat went into convulsions, the others avoided the poison; they connected death to its source. The experimenters diluted the poison so that its killing effect took several days, and large swarms of rats were killed. The rats couldn't connect death with its source.

If Americans could identify the problem of the schools, they would make the necessary changes, but like the diluted poison, its source is *indiscernable*.

Every institution has its critics who cause uncomfortable irritations. But the public school is facing more than critics, she is fighting for her existential life, under attack, and suffering erosion from within and onslaughts of enemies from without. George Washington's starved Revolutionary army may have defeated the larger armies of England, but do the public schools of America have the necessary courage to stand the tests of oppression?

The Failures of the Public Schools

The public schools have many shortcomings. These failures are sometimes caused by change in educational policy. At other times, their failure is the *result* of inefficient education. The following fifteen problems are an indictment against the public schools. Each has a vicious face. Just as "beauty lies in the beholder's eyes," so an ugly threat is measured by one's understanding of the public school's failure. The list varies with different authorities, and all of the failures are interwoven. Some of these failures are self-inflicted. The public schools have brought the problems on their heads. Other problems are polluting education, even though their origin can't be blamed on public school educators. Mrs. Saxon Bargeron, Superintendent of Chatham-Savannah, Georgia, schools, lists the five top charges leveled at public schools: Lack of discipline, busing, rising costs, poor teachers, and low student achievement. The Gallop poll lists the problems as seen by response to their questions in 1973.[2]

1. Lack of discipline
2. Integration/segregation problems
3. Lack of proper financial support
4. Difficulty of getting "good" teachers
5. Use of drugs
6. Size of school/classes
7. Poor curriculum
8. Parents' lack of interest
9. Lack of proper facilities
10. School board policies

The following list is offered as a view of the problems of the public schools. Possibly it will give the reader a comprehensive view of the charges brought against the public schools.

1. *The untimely invasion by courts into educational matters.* The courts have overthrown the historic precedent of local educational control. The process began innocently enough when school boards and districts were consolidated to provide bigger and larger schools. But in the process, parents had less to say about their schools, and educators felt less responsible to a local clientele. As school districts grew larger in metropolitan areas, apathy

gripped the communities' ability to deal with educational abuses.

When the Supreme Court declared segregation unconstitutional, local school boards once again lost control of their districts. Federal judges have continued the process, not only determining who goes where to school, but also have blocked dress codes, expulsions, and expressions of religious heritage.

In the last decade, there has been a decline in the number of public school boards from 25,000 to 18,000.

2. *The deterioration of educational purposes.* Low standards and changed goals are the often heard charge against the public schools. The *Minneapolis Tribune* says of the students from a progressive school:

Probably the most serious development is that some of the students have become worried whether they are learning basic skills and normal school subjects . . . they are at a point where they want skilled teachers rather than groovy relators.

The whole thrust in education today maintains, "We teach students, we don't teach subjects." This is bunk. The acid test of education is the student. How good is he? How well can he produce? A student may be well rounded, but if he does not know his subject, he is not educated. When a teacher asks his pupils, "What are your needs?" as a basis of the curriculum, the teacher is moving in a purposeless circle.

Dr. John R. Miles, writing in the new quarterly edition of the *Saturday Evening Post* (Spring 1972) said:

The nation's number one academic problem in education today is a reading problem. The U. S. office of education has estimated, there are 24 million people 18 years old or older in the United States who are functionally illiterate.

That means they cannot read, write, or count well enough to handle the day-to-day tasks demanded of them in a modern society . . . yet, it isn't because they haven't gone to school . . . the vast majority of those 24 million "functionally illiterate" people had gone to school for at least five years, but learned little except to hate school.

Without authority, the public schools don't know where they are going. They have assumed that truth is relative, and like the gypsy can change with each community and adapt itself to each culture, so truth is vacillating, always changing.

Students in New York City and Plainfield, New Jersey, successfully demonstrated for lower grade requirements for student counsel candidates so more black students could participate. An observer noted, "These children of the outside demand that the school community be shared with them."

Because of the public school's drift to socialization, many schools are appearing anti-intellectual. The new cry is heard, "Why can't Johnny add?" Headmaster Bill Meeks of Jonesco Academy in Gray, Georgia, who last year left a 20-year public school career, indicates there is a waiting line for his school. He notes, "Our school is like the public schools used to be." Meeks was previously a public high school principal in Macon, Georgia.[3]

3. *The student is reduced to a high-grade animal.* The public schools no longer recognize that man was created in the image of God. Public school textbooks do not recognize that man has a soul-spirit, nor conscious existence that lives on after death. The Christian view is not even recognized as one of the explanations for the nature of man.

Students are treated as high-grade animals, but edu-

cators will not recognize their animal nature. They hold
man is inherently good, which he is. But a proper view of
human nature recognizes both negative and constructive
forces within the pupil. A proper view of personality rec-
onciles the Jekyll/Hyde nature of man, that he is both
good and bad at the same time.

If psychology only ignored the existence of the soul
and educated in the traditional pattern, these would be
little problems. But educators are growing in their commitment to "behavior modification." A student is changed
and shaped by a system of rewards, recognizing him for
acceptable behavior and ignoring behavior which is unacceptable. Based on experiments by Russian Ivan Pav-
lov, this means behavior is changed apart from rational
processes. It is pure behaviorism. Educators are turning
from education of the mind, the process of broadening
the intellect and of increasing powers to evaluate, understand, interpret, and choose. They treat our children as
high-grade animals.

The method is more than bribery, it is anti-intellectual
at core. But educators are reinforced by the knowledge
that it works. "Behavior modification" is pure brainwashing at best, or rats running through a maze at worst.

One of the leading advocates, B.F. Skinner, the Harvard psychologist, feels man is a product of his environment. As such he can be controlled. His thoughts and
actions can be controlled. Questions immediately come to
mind: "Who will control our students? To what end are
they controlled?"

Historically, education recognized the immaterial nature of man, that he had a soul. In an effort to get rid of
the supernatural, the soul was eliminated. The child was
told he had a spirit. Next, educators got rid of the spirit

and viewed the pupils' internal nature as *self*. Now man has lost his self and must seek "self-identity." Many parents do not want this form of education. Education has historically made its students free, but when the true nature of man is ignored, education is a tool used by the schools to control its students.

4. *The public schools are a socio-political tool to solve social injustices.* The *Atlanta Journal* ran an article, "All-White Academies, for Learning or Segregation?" quoting a cynic who calls them "segregation academies." J.R. Rhodes, Sr., Chairman of the Board of Baker Academy at Newton, Georgia, explains the reason for establishing the school in 1970, "It was just a situation whereby some of the people wanted the children to have a choice—an all-white school or an integrated school. And that's the reason we established the school: to give them freedom of choice." [4] One state department official estimated that half of the 284 private schools listed by the Georgia Department of Education were segregation academies.

Racial segregation is an injustice; but at the same time, forced busing also produces injustices. The family who sacrifices to live in a better neighborhood so that the children can have a superior education suffers racial injustice in reverse. Few white families resent black children attending their neighborhood school. Most desire the black family to get the best education possible, even if black children are bused from their neighborhood to white communities.

Most educators realize now that the issue of forced busing is not primarily a racial issue. Parents don't want their children bused into a high crime district where their children are exposed to violence, rape, extortion, and second-rate education.[5] If a family pays higher taxes, it should have access to better education. In the American ethic, we have approved a man's purchasing what he can afford. The man who drives a Cadillac and lives in a poor neighborhood apparently does not value education as much as the man who drives a Volkswagen and invests more of his income in a higher-priced home.

A public opinion poll indicated that 86 percent of Americans replied, "No!" to the question, "Do you favor busing children to solve problems of racial imbalance?" America is a nation that depends on democratic rule. Yet the opinion of the majority is neglected. Bureaucrats have determined that the schools will be used to solve a social problem. Our schools have entered a non-educational realm and have attempted to correct social problems through forced busing; hence increasing the financial load of taxpayers, administrative burdens of school officials, plus adding to the logistical problems caused by busing. Against the will of 86 percent of our people, children from Washington, D.C. to Los Angeles, California, are being transported millions of miles from their local community.

The *San Francisco Times* indicated last spring, "Busing is dormant as an issue." In Chinatown, the "Freedom Schools" were organized by Chinese parents who opposed busing in 1971. Dr. Dennis Wong, one of the organizers, answered the question why Chinese parents opposed busing from their neighborhood schools. "It's the same old question, the quality and the quantity of education and the safety for Chinese students," said Wong, noting, "Parents are not opposed to integration *per se* . . . there's still a lot of violence."

5. *The Supreme Court ruling which forced prayer and Bible reading out of public schools*. The opening portion

of the First Amendment to the Constitution established a line of separation between the church and state.

Congress shall make no law respecting an establishment of religion, or prohibiting the free exercise thereof . . .

Religious liberty was extended to all states by the Fourteenth Amendment. These two amendments prohibit Congress, any state legislature, local school board, or any school authority (including teachers) from establishing any religious practice in the public schools. The effect of the Supreme Court decision is that Bible reading and/or recitation of the Lord's Prayer or any other officially composed prayer, when required by school authorities, is a violation of the First Amendment of the Constitution. The author agrees with these decisions for the following reasons: (1) Required Bible reading and prayer could be the beginning of a state religion. (2) Required Bible reading and prayer when conducted on a sectarian basis violates the rights of a minority. (3) If I support religious exercise when it agrees with my opinion, I am obligated to support religious exercise when I am in a minority. (4) If Bible reading and prayer were required by the public school, then religious exercises would be led by those who are spiritually unqualified. A teacher might be praying to a God he doesn't recognize. (5) Any religious exercise will lead to dead formalism if not attached to commitment or persuasion. Since the public school cannot attempt to win converts to Jesus Christ, the religious exercises would lead to pseudo-Christianity or dead orthodoxy. (6) Religious exercises in the public schools will emphasize commonality of faith, pushing churches toward an ecumenical world church.

However, critics who drive religion out of the public

schools also are attacking the Protestant/Puritan ethic (see chapter seven). Since an ethic is a catalyst of society, any aggressive campaign against the Protestant/Puritan ethic will have an adverse effect on the nation.

Robert Havinghurst from the University of Chicago stated, "There has emerged within the past ten years a set of values and behaviors which have been called the *counterculture*." He notes, "The American society is going through pervasive and fundamental value changes." [6] A new religion of secularism is emerging. Dr. Carl S.F. Henry told a national symposium, sponsored by the Public Education Religious Studies Center, at Wright State University, "It is not the establishment of a sectarian religion in the traditional sense, but the educational disestablishment of such religion in favor of a religion of secularism that presently reflects the pulsebeat of much education in the public arena." [7]

Carl Henry noted, in the June 1973 meeting, "The threat of religious establishment in the United States today comes not from any form of Biblical faith—Protestant, Catholic, or Jewish—but from secular humanism."

"Atheists have taken over public education in the United States," charged Dr. Weldon Shoftstall, Arizona's Superintendent of Public Education. Speaking at the dedication of a new science and music building of Phoenix Christian High School, Dr. Shoftstall said, "Public schools are becoming more and more atheistic . . . because of poor grade confusion . . . a belief that religion is exclusively a personal matter, a belief that separation of church and state includes separation of religion and education, and acceptance of collectivism in the name of individualism, and an acceptance of humanism as theism." Shoftstall noted that atheism is synonymous with humanism, and commented, "Many Christians seem to feel humanism is a respectable philosophy." He noted that humanism is actually the worship of man.

The public schools should not indoctrinate sectarian Christianity, but also should not swing to the opposite extreme of indoctrinating sectarian humanism. The following practices could be incorporated in the public schools.[9]

(1) The use of the Bible as a reference book in teaching secular subjects.

(2) The study of the Bible for its literary and historic qualities.

(3) The study of comparative religion and the history of religion, especially as it relates to the advancement of civilization.

(4) The recitation of historical documents such as the Declaration of Independence, which contains references to God.

(5) The singing of the National Anthem and other patriotic hymns which profess the composer's faith in God.

(6) References to God on patriotic or ceremonial occasions.

(7) The excusing of students from classes for participation in worship services.

To the above seven legal practices, the author would add:

(8) Recognition of the Protestant/Puritan ethic as the basis for the American value system.

6. *The decline of discipline in the process of education.* The Gallup Poll indicates lack of discipline was the major criticism Americans levelled against their public schools in the years 1960 to 1973.[10] The editors concluded, "The

greatest complaint against the schools—is lack of discipline." In trying to explain the cause for public concern the editors concluded, "Lack of proper discipline is often associated . . . with poor education." [11]

Discipline is the basic means to acquire skills, content, and attitude. In an attempt to make learning enjoyable and meet pupil needs, educators have sought to eliminate drudgery from education. However, they seem to have swung to nihilism and hedonism.

In 1972, when the Gallup Poll asked Americans to choose from a list of nine goals of public schools, the public placed at the top of the list, "Teaching students to respect law and authority." [12]

The champions of new math argued that children could learn arithmetic by insight and problem solving. But the majority of students who have taken "new math" score lower in ability to do arithmetic when compared with students who have learned by traditional means. Therefore, critics of new math are hoping for a swing back toward drill.

Howard J. Hausman of the National Science Foundation stated, "Modern math clearly requires superior teaching . . . but if you stake the average child's learning on his having superior teaching, he won't learn." An editorial in the *Lynchburg News* (Virginia) indicates, "The average person electing to go into public school teaching is by every intellectual intent inferior to the college student preparing for other professions." [13] The editorial claims that children do poorer in arithmetic because of poor teachers.

Not only is discipline being forced out of academic subjects, administrators have not advocated sensible external controls over their school. Spineless educators are unwilling to enforce the rules that are left. The old adage still is true: "A school teacher is a man among boys, and a boy among men."

Realizing that pressure brings about maturity, some public school educators are giving second thoughts to the priorities of work and discipline. Michael Mallory calls the high school ""Just an aging vat" in the *New York Times:*

The trouble with kids nowadays is they spend too much time sitting on their tails in school rooms. Send them out to make a buck, rub them up against the real world for a change and maybe they will stop a lot of their foolishness.[14]

Mallory claims this is not "Archie Bunker" speaking, but what heavyweight educators are saying about the American high schools. He opposes the school-till-sixteen rule, but indicates it probably will remain a national law.

Dr. James Becker of the National Foundation for the Improvement of Education notices the lack of discipline and observes: "We may have ruined a whole generation of kids in terms of learning what the responsibility of a citizen is in terms of work." [15]

7. *Increased teacher unionization, teacher militancy, senseless strikes, and compulsory teacher-Board of Education negotiations.* For many years the schoolteacher was considered a second-class citizen in the community. With much hard work, the role of public schoolteacher has risen to a professional status. Now incipit unionism is reducing teachers to the level of blue-collar factory workers. The Gallup Poll indicates, "Another cancer the American public has about the schools relates to the growing militancy of teachers." [16]

In the past, the National Education Association lobbied

in Washington and the state capitals. The thought of a teacher strike was abhorrent. In an article, "The Five Most Cited Reasons for Faculty Unionism," Lindeman, Assistant to the Academic Vice President, University of Guam, noted: (1) Inadequate compensation, (2) dissatisfaction with faculty role in government, (3) the statutory right to bargain, (4) inept administration, and (5) competition for membership among the NEA, AFT and other teacher organizations.[17]

Teachers should have the right to join unions. The Gallup Poll indicates: "The public generally agrees that teachers should have the right to form unions. At the same time, a majority of the public is against permitting teachers to strike."[18] If controlled properly, unions can make a necessary contribution to the process of education in public schools. But one of the harmful effects of teachers' unions is their desire to obtain a virtual monopoly over school policy, curriculum, and finances. The conservative columnist, Russell Kirk, in an editorial entitled "Public Schools Becoming Agencies of Political Power," wrote: "The unions are trying to thrust aside the duly constituted school authorities—the local school board." He quoted a young union leader who said, "Teachers should band together against school boards who are their natural enemies." Even though teachers claim they are striking for the welfare of children, only the naïve believe them. In a union battle, the victims are always the pupils.

David Selden, the national president of the American Federation of Teachers, demanded that teachers engage in statewide bargaining. This virtually ignores the local school boards. In effect, unions are separating schools farther from parents and local communities.

If the National Education Association and the American Federation of Teachers merge, parents will be confronted by a virtual monopoly of their public schools. Education will be in the hands of a politically-biased union, and parents will have less to say about their schools than they do now. When that happens, parents will put their children in private schools. I am not against teacher unions; I am against them killing the public schools and thereby causing the collapse of freedom.

8. *The drug and narcotic problem in the public schools.* A drug epidemic has exploded in the public schools, leaving human wreckage in its fallout. Students are afraid, authorities are intimidated, and many parents have grave doubts about sending their children to public schools. Dr. Paul Kienel, Director of the California Association of Christian Schools, quoted a conversation where he was told 50 percent of all high school students and 30 percent of elementary students in New York City are on drugs of some kind.[19] In the same newsletter, he cited young girls who were afraid to go to the girls' rest room for an entire day because of potential violence.

Narcotics and drugs are problems that cannot be directly attributed to the public schools. Nevertheless, it is a problem they must encounter. The only reason some parents refuse to send their children to public schools is to protect them from drugs.

The Gallup Poll revealed that Americans are deeply concerned with the traffic of drugs in the public school, listing it fifth in their order of concern.[20]

9. *Uncontrolled violence.* Violence has become a way of life in public schools, almost as predictable as recess or vacations. Statistics on violence are not reliable inasmuch

as some acts are not reported by students, other acts that are reported to the office are not recorded, and some acts are hushed up by school officials.

Rudolph Jezek, Principal of Barten Elementary School, Chicago, was shot dead behind his own desk.[21]

Stephen Guy, a 14-year-old pupil with a history of disciplinary troubles, walked calmly past four clerks to the principal's windowless office. He drew a .45 caliber automatic weapon and said, "I don't want to be transferred to Mosely." After he killed Jezek, the student shot Ezekiel Thomas, a security guard, and Assistant Principal Gordon Sharp. Guy burst in on his homeroom teacher, Peter Smith, but the teacher escaped into the hall, with his pupil firing at him. Finally another teacher pinned the killer-pupil to the floor.

Stephen Guy had previously threatened a teacher with a chair, and, according to school officials, needed help. He was being transferred to another school because of overcrowding.

This one act of violence could be a misrepresentation of the public schools, but it's happened too often to ignore. Whose is the blame in school violence? asked the *Chicago Daily News.* Robert Billings, reporter, asked, "The system's? Society's? The school board's? The changing neighborhood's? The gang's? The parents'?" Placing blame is difficult in any one isolated case. Some accuse the public school for instigating the violence, others blame them for allowing permissiveness that breeds defiance of laws. Whether the public schools are guilty of indirectly inciting violence, or whether violence is the by-product of public schools, no one can deny the violence that festers around our classrooms. As a result, quality education suffers, and parents are taking their children to private schools.

10. *Public schools are guilty of book burning.* Modern educators do not actually light fires, but in practice they have made the same decisions as ancient book burners. Public schools are guilty of censorship.[22] In reality, every individual exercises some form of censorship every day of his life. He rejects one TV program in favor of another; he purchases one paperback in the local newspaper stand, while rejecting several. When a speaker infuriates him, he simply turns off the radio.

Censorship usually means prohibiting expression. Censorship is prohibiting an individual from writing or speaking his opinion. If the opinion is already given, censorship involves suppressing the message. The public school has censored religious books and the Bible from its classroom. Also it has excluded divine creation as an alternate explanation for the origin of the universe. Educators give lip service to objectivity, yet they damage their professionalism by refusing to include any contrary opinions in their curriculum. Hence, public schools are just as guilty of burning books as John Calvin was in burning the works of Cervantes in the streets of Geneva.

While censoring religious material (that has historically been taught in the classroom), authorities allow questionable pornography to be freely taught in the public schools.

A concerned Macon, Georgia mother, pulled her 16-year-old daughter out of the public school in May 1973 because a teacher assigned a "dirty" book to read. The book, *Man Child in the Promised Land* by Claude Brown, describes life in Harlem, explicitly depicting sexual scenes. The mother told the *Atlanta Journal,* "It's nothing but pure vulgar sex and filth." [23]

The teacher defended her action, claiming, "The events are part of everyday life in Harlem."

"It may be part of everyday life in Harlem . . . but it's not part of everyday life around here," replied the irate mother.

Is Censorship Intolerant?

Some educators claim that a ban on books is ineffective and that censorship is intolerant. But we are not talking about banning books or suppressing publication. The issue is requiring impressionable young minds to read profanity, immorality, filth, and other materials undermining confidence in the American way of life. An assignment to read a filthy book is not the same as indoctrination, but impressionable minds have difficulty forgetting what they read. The child is still the sum total of all of his experiences.

11. *Ignoring standards of deportment, dress codes, and behavior.* In refusing to deal with dress codes and behavior, educators have neglected a primary educational principle, i.e. the outer man reflects the inner. But the responsibility does not rest solely with public schools. Judges have handed down decisions that handcuff school administrators. The Gallup Poll reflects the helplessness of administrators: court rulings have not helped the discipline situation.[24]

Principal J.R. Reynolds of Herschel V. Jenkins High School in Savannah, Georgia, held up his hands in despair during an interview, indicating there was nothing be could do about students' dress. "If I phone home and the mother approves of her child's dress, there's nothing

I can do." The Gallup Poll indicates court rulings have almost ended the *loco parent* in principle.[25]

High School Unrest, published in 1969, indicated that the major cause of student protest was dress and grooming. It stated, "The miniskirted girl and the long-haired boy were usually at the center of those episodes." [26] In a survey taken by the National Association of Secondary School Principals, 82 percent of the schools reported protests came under fire because of school rules.

Goodbye to Cleanliness!

The cleanliness ethic is no longer valued. There was a time when public school teachers exhorted their students to wash their hands, clean their face, and brush their teeth. Today the torch of truth is held high by the hands of the shabby and unkept.

12. *Public confidence in their schools is eroding.* The cost of education is going up, while voter resistance hardens. Americans are losing faith in their public schools and it's not just a high cost of financing them. Americans are willing to pay the price for projects they believe in. Today they question the public schools.

In 1973, Governor Ronald Reagan of California addressed the National Association of Secondary School Principals in Anaheim, California:

In California, the total enrollment growth in grade kindergarten through twelve has been only 7.2 percent over the past six budget years. Yet, the state alone has increased its support for kindergarten through 12 by 45% in that same period.

Reagan then asked the principals, "The public asks why more and more money is needed to educate fewer and fewer children?"

Financiers estimate that the $90 billion spent on public schools each year is as much as the rest of the world put together spends on education. Yet high school graduates have difficulty reading the diplomas they are handed at their commencement exercise!

Perhaps the public is feeling the revolutionary mood of those who dumped tea into the Boston Harbor, crying, "No taxation without representation!" When parents have less to say about what goes on in their schools, they are less willing to make the sacrifice for their schools.

A bond issue in Fairfax, Virginia, failed in June 1972. As a result, Judy Nash, Principal of Freedom Hill Elementary School, indicated the old furnace is so uncontrollable that one classroom may be nearly 40 degrees hotter than the next.[27] Mrs. Judy Pirnie, a teacher's aid, holds math class in the hallway. Yet the community did not approve a bond issue, where $1 million goes to Freedom Hill, $7.5 goes to Groveton High School, and $5.1 goes for new elementary schools. Perhaps voters balked at carpeted floors, new auto mechanics shop, music rooms, and other fringe benefits unrelated to the core of education. No one can adequately understand voter resistance, but the public school must live with it. They have lost the confidence of the communities they serve.

The Gallup Poll in 1969 revealed that lack of proper facilities was the second major problem listed by the public regarding their schools. Within four years the problem has dropped to ninth on a list of ten alternatives. The public no longer is concerned with better facilities. When asked, "Do you think additional expenditure of money makes a great deal of difference in the achievement or progress of students?" only 30 percent now say "Yes." The Gallup Poll predicts:

Just as some studies have shown that student achievement is not closely related to class size, so some other studies have shown that the amount of money spent per child . . . bears little relationship to the child's progress in school. . . . This research will almost certainly be a factor in future consideration of the financial needs of the public schools.[28]

With the growing taxpayer rebellion against new taxes and the defeat of school bond referendums educators began shopping around for new ways to finance public education. Property tax, the traditional keystone of education, has carried the burden. However, federal support from Washington began breaking into the picture in the early 60's. Most educators didn't question the source of money or its control, they just spent it. But with federal money came a breakup of "local control." Parents have less to say about education today, and Washington has more control than at any time in the history of the United States.

13. *Public school bureaucracy creates inefficiency and alienation.* The public school system has become a bureaucracy with all of its inherent weaknesses. As the machine gets larger, bureaucracy builds alienation into employees, cutting morale and efficiency. Hence, an inefficient school system needs more employees, demanding more tax money. All the while, work output is reduced.

The fruit of bureaucracy is punctiliousness and secretiveness concerning the affairs of the organization. Employees become apathetic to the goal of public schools. Just as pressure in a machine produces friction, bureaucracy produces friction among individuals, disenchantment with ideals, alienation, and personal atrophy.

Dedication is still found in many classroom teachers, but the spread of unionism might corrupt their emotional commitment to teaching. Bureaucracy could be another nail hammered into the coffin of the public schools.

14. *The erosion of respect within the educational community.* When an institution no longer has self-respect, it comes unglued. The casual observer of the public school senses the dissolvement of school pride. Buildings are defaced. Anything not nailed down is ripped off. Glass is broken. Trash is strewn through the halls. Pupils don't take seriously their role as learners. Many don't value an education. They are simply putting in time.

15. *The counterrevolutionary Christian school movement.* The public school has many failures. Some failures might bring more wrath on the schools than other shortcomings. But the growth of the Christian school movement is the strongest indictment against the public schools.

The public school movement is the foundation of freedom within the United States. It built our nation. Now there is a revolutionary force within our schools, tearing them apart. This revolution has been described within this chapter. Now the Christian schools are counterrevolutionary. Christian schools are more than a blue collar backlash against busing. Christian schools are more than a few Fundamentalists wanting to keep their children in a "ghetto mentality." The counterrevolutionary Christian schools are attempting to reestablish the original American value system. The success of these schools will syphon off more students into private education. When a cycle begins to run its course, the movement from a high-pressure area into a vacuum increases the momentum. If the better students enroll in Christian schools, the quality of public education will drop. As a result, more pupils will seek private education. Also, if parents who are most concerned about their children send them to private schools, who will support the public schools? Without community backing, bureaucratic fungus will spread throughout the public school system, further deteriorating the whole process.

As enrollment drops in the public schools, a smaller school enrollment cannot justify larger financial expenditures. Lawmakers will cut back appropriations. Hence, the cycle of deterioration will increase.

Have the public schools had it? Only the resident of the future will know. If they continue in their present course, the public schools are finished.

Like a river flood sweeping everything in its path to onrushing destruction, the public schools have consumed the children of our nation and made them a part of its system. The fact that schools have changed doesn't seem to bother those within the onrushing flood, they are too caught up in its stream to notice the ultimate destination. And as every flood plays itself out, so the public school may die by its own making. Death comes because of: (1) court decisions, (2) anti-intellectualism, (3) reducing man to a high-grade animal, (4) becoming a sociopolitical tool, (5) forced evacuation of the secular, (6) the decline of discipline, (7) increased teacher unionization, (8) drugs, (9) uncontrolled violence, (10) book burning, (11) refusing to deal with character development, (12) erosion of public confidence, (13) incipient educational bureaucracy, and (14) emasculated educational pride. Finally, (15) the emergence of counterrevolutionary schools will spyhon off the final cohesive elements of the public schools, increasing the downward cycle to ultimate death.

NOTES

1. As quoted by Ann Marshall in *Savannah Morning News,* Savannah, Georgia, November 20, 1973, p. D-1.

2. *The Gallup Polls of Attitudes Toward Education, 1969-1973,* Ed Stanley Elam (Bloomington, Indiana: *Phi Delta Kappa,* 1973) p. 153.

3. As quoted by Steve Stewart in *The Atlanta Journal,* Atlanta, Georgia, July 1, 1973, p. 20-A.

4. *Ibid.*

5. The Gallup Poll supports this view stating, "The two—integration and busing—should not be confused. While busing is one way to bring about integration, polls have consistently shown an overwhelming majority of Americans opposed to achieving integration." p. 166. *The Gallup Polls of Attitudes Toward Education 1969-1973,* edited by Stanley Elam (Bloomington, Indiana: *Phi Delta Kappa,* 1973) p. 166. This attitude has remained consistent for the past five years.

6. Robert Havighurst, "Human Development, Societal Changes and Adult Moral Character," *Religious Education,* (LXVIII), May-June, 1973, p. 407.

7. Quoted from a release by Religious News Service as printed in *Tulsa Herald All-Church Press,* p. 5.

8. Quoted from a release by Religious News Service as printed in *Tulsa Herald All-Church Press.* (Vol. 44, No. 10) November 4, 1973, p. 4.

9. James V. Panoch and David L. Barr, *Religion Goes to School,* (New York: Harper and Row, Publisher, 1968). An excellent summary of opinion of religion in the public schools.

10. Gallup Polls, p. 14, 153.

11. *Ibid.,* p. 14.

12. *Ibid.,* p. 157

13. Editorial, "Education In Spite Of" *The News,* Lynchburg, Virginia, May 30, 1973, p. A-6.

14. Michael T. Malloy, "U. S. High Schools: Just An Aging

Vat," *The New York Times,* (Vol. 12, No. 41), October 13, 1973, p. 1.

15. *Ibid.*

16. *Gallup Poll,* p. 3.

17. Lynn Williams Lindeman, "The Five Most Cited Reasons for Faulty Unionization," *Intellect* (November, 1973) p. 85.

18. *Gallup Poll,* p. 3.

19. Paul A. Kienel, Executive Director of California Association of Christian Schools, *Christian School Comment* (Vol. 3, No. 4).

20. *Gallup Poll,* p. 56, 152.

21. As reported by Robert Billings, *Chicago Daily News,* Chicago, Illinois, January 18, 1974, p. 6.

22. F. C. Ellenbury, "Phantasy and Facts, Censorship and Schools," *The Clearing House,* (Vol 45, No. 9), May 1971, p. 515-519. The article does not accuse the public schools of censorship, but claims schools must be open to knowledge. Yet, applying this criterion, the schools are rejecting Christian influence.

23. As quoted for *The Atlanta Journal,* Atlanta, Georgia, "Teachers' Book Choice Challenged," July 14, 1973, p. 2.

24. *Gallup Poll,* p. 2.

25. *Ibid.*

26. *High School Student Unrest,* National School Public Relations Association, 1201 Sixteenth Street, Washington, D. C. 20036, p. 2.

27. Thomas W. Love, *The Fairfax Star-News,* Fairfax, Virginia, December 22, 1973, p. 2.

28. *Gallup Poll,* p. 159.

3 A Protest Come of Age

The reasons parents enroll their children in private schools are as different as a person's aim for living. Some private schools with tradition appeal to blue blood aristocrats who want their children to get the refinement of finishing school, the academic challenge of a college preparatory course, or to get the discipline of a military school. Some new Southern academies are segregationist schools. Parents don't want their kids educated with blacks. Other new academies were founded to keep kids from being bused across town. Parents fear violence or pseudo-education for their kids. Other new private schools emphasize Americanism and patriotism.

Among religious schools, the Roman Catholics have the largest system with 10,770 schools, and 2,808,000 pupils.

Growth in the private school movement is measured among non-religious schools which increased by 90.8 percent, and Protestant schools which grew by 46.1 percent. Enrollment in Roman Catholic schools decreased by 19.3 percent in the past ten years.

The Protestant private schools are by no means monolithic. They differ in purpose and structure. They are basically four types of schools: (1) parochial, (2) parent society, (3) inter-denominational, and (4) local church sponsored Christian schools. *Parochial* means "one's own"

and is a school sponsored for the education of the children of the sponsoring church, such as Catholics, who
have 10,770 schools, and Adventists, who have 658
schools. A *parent society* school is controlled and administered by a board of trustees who are elected by a society
of parents. The Christian Reformed Church,[1] with 294
schools, has been educating its children for over 100 years
through societies because they believe Scripture teaches
parents have the responsibility to educate their children.
The National Association of Christian Schools is made up
of 313 schools, usually *interdenominational* in control and
outreach. State associations such as the California Association of Christian Schools have increased from 68 member schools to 308 in the past seven years. However, some
of the schools in these organizations are interdenominational, while others are local church sponsored. The *local
church sponsored* schools are controlled by a local congregation and usually meet in the educational facilities of
that church even though their doors are open to the entire community. They believe the Lord gave the church
the authority, "teaching them to observe all things whatsoever I have said unto you" (Matthew 28:20). This
means both Sunday School and day school education.
The American Association of Christian Schools is reflective
of this group. The explosive growth of private Christian
schools is occurring mostly in local church schools although only about 1,000 of them are associated in any
way with the American Association of Christian Schools.

A Parent Society School

"Schools for Christian Education in Holland, Michigan,"
is the name given to one parent society which is composed of 1,260 families in this western Michigan town of

40,000 population. The Society controls three elementary, one middle, and one high school, with a total enrollment of 2,500 pupils. The schools grew out of the Christian Reformed Church in 1902 and have grown yearly. However, as the Christian school movement has exploded in growth, the Holland Christian Schools have experienced a slight decline for no other reason than theology. They believe parents should provide education, and, as birth rate declines, parents are not having as many children, hence enrollment was down four percent last year. The association is open for membership to all those who have children enrolled in the school or to the interested public, and a high percentage attend the two yearly meetings of the society. From these parents, fifteen men are chosen to serve on a Board of Trustees which: (1) approves all teachers; (2) governs finances; (3) approves expulsions, and; (4) determines educational policy. Over 90 percent of students come from the Christian Reformed Church.[2] Those who come from outside the denomination choose its schools for its quality education. Holland, Michigan does not have busing or an ethnic problem in its public schools; therefore, middle-class Americans have not fled its public schools.

The Holland Christian High School is valued over $2 million and was constructed at $12.00 a sq. ft. It is as modern as any public school. Most of the tradesmen were Christian Reformed, and superior craftsmanship is evident. These workers donated what one teacher called in the Dutch vernacular "a labor of love."

The immaculate terrazzo floors are cleaner than the day the building was dedicated. After each of the seven daily class changes, the janitors come out with their long brooms and sweep the halls, picking up the seldom dropped trash. No locks are on the lockers. Vice-Principal Arthur Wyma indicates, "Thus far, our students respect personal property, and petty thievery is almost non-existent." The visitor is amazed not to see lockers scraped, marked, or bent out of shape.

Six women from town still provide a hot lunch for 35 cents including meat, vegetables; they bake rolls, cookies, and all the desserts.

Walking into the gym, Wyma says, "This is the biggest gym in town; when we built, we wanted to do it right." The automated bleachers were provided by parent associations.

Walking into the band room, the observer sees the walls lined with award plaques won by the high school band. The band represented Michigan in the Presidential Inaugural Parade, 1969. The motto on the wall announces, "Results, not excuses."

Parents wanted to provide for the total education of their children. There are tennis courts, three baseball diamonds, a soccer field, and five acres of woods for biology and tree planting experiments.

Parents felt the library ought not to be just another room; therefore, they approved plans calling for a large cathedral ceiling, carpet, and walls filled with volumes, a token of their dedication to "book learning."

Almost 100 percent of the biology students over the years have sold magazines throughout the city, financing equipment for educational endeavors. The biology teacher points with pride to 36 microscopes supplied by students. The school's greenhouse has a plaque, "A dynamic token of the loyalty of all biology students who participated in nine annual magazine sales." However, the signs of the times are infiltrating the school: the first indication of student lawlessness came when panes were broken from the greenhouse.

Superintendent of Holland Christian Schools, Marvin Essenburg's Ph.D. dissertation compared Christian Reformed schools with public schools in the North Central Accrediting Association, indicating students from Christian schools scored approximately one year above the public schools on standardized tests.

Historically, Protestants have ignored elementary and secondary education, but have been committed to Christian education at the college level. Known as the "Inverted Pyramid," all Christian emphasis comes at the end of the process. Christian Reformed educators charge other Protestant denominations with being inconsistent in their philosophy of education. They believe the concept of Christian education should stretch from kindergarten through college. As one visits Holland, Michigan, or other similar communities, he is aware of the Dutch subculture. One might ask the question, "Does the Dutch subculture continue because of their Christian schools?"

Superintendent Essenburg indicates the public school is not normative education. Something is missing. "We don't just add a Bible course or give students the influence of a Christian teacher." The principal indicates, "The Christian school is education as it should be." Perhaps teaching out of one of the most consistent philosophies, the parent society schools feel the physical sciences cannot be properly based only on evolution. A child must understand creation. The social sciences cannot be understood apart from the providence of God; man cannot solve his problems only through counseling. The power of God to change the life is the basis of all student growth. Essenburg believes the public schools are not able to teach the ultimate purpose in life. He maintains every student should live to the glory of God.

Essenburg maintains, "The greatest challenge is to teach as God would have us teach . . ." The Christian teacher is the key to the success of Holland Christian Schools. Most of the teachers are from Christian colleges. When asked if a Baptist could teach in their schools, Essenburg indicated that question is not now being raised.[3] But, he pointed out, it was not his decision. Parents make the decisions as to who shall teach their children through the Board of Trustees. However, all teachers must be thoroughly Calvinist in doctrine and live an exemplary life as taught by the Christian Reformed Church. There is little teacher turnover in the system. In 1973, only three new teachers were employed in the system that now has 100 employees.

The school has few rules and regulations. In the Christian Reformed Church parents are responsible for the dress of the children. Therefore, the schools are not expected to speak out on clothing or standards.[3] Essenburg indicated, "Too often other Protestants expect their church or school to enforce a standard because the home cannot or will not."

The Assistant Principal in charge of discipline indicated, "We can phone home and be quite sure of backing in our discipline." Last year there were no permanent expulsions although a couple of students left the school because of their general dislike for the kind of education they were getting.

Years ago, the high school was accredited by The North Central Association of Colleges and Secondary Schools which pressured the high school to include home economics and vocational shop. The resolute parents gave up accreditation rather than compromise their dedication to academic excellence. Not one student had difficulty in getting into college because of the school's academic reputation.

In the old days, many surrounding communities organized "bus societies" to transport their children to the Holland school. The families of one "bus society" unloaded boxcars, donating their pay to transport children to school. Today, the school provides bus transportation to schools.

An Interdenominational School

The interdenominational Christian Schools rode the growing crest of the interdenominational wave between 1950 to 1970. They reflected the mood of cooperation among evangelicals in such movements as Youth for Christ, the National Sunday School Association, and interdenominational Christian colleges. Those who felt a need for day-to-day Christian education formed self-perpetuating boards to control and perpetuate a Christian school. Funds and students were recruited on a non-sectarian basis. The movement has been stable but not aggressive, often plagued by inadequate facilities, low budgets, and high teacher turnover. With all of its handicaps, the movement has stressed quality education, integrity of character, and high standards.

Brethren Christian School, a pre-kindergarten through grade 12 interdenominational school of 350 pupils, serves the Michiana area of Northern Indiana (South Bend, Elkhart, Osceola, and Southern Michigan). The high school meets in old Christian education facilities of Bethel Brethren Church, Osceola, a typical midwestern church, a few blocks off a main railroad line. Located two miles away on 20 acres is the modern concrete block elementary school where 200 students meet in eight classes. A new $150,000 gym is used jointly by the elementary and secondary schools. Administrator David Miller said 35 percent of the county is Catholic. Nationally-known Notre Dame University is located 15 miles away. The administrator indicated 27 private schools were operating in the county, of which 21 are Catholic. His is the oldest and largest Christian High School. Other non-public schools are Baptist, Mennonite, Pentecostal, and an exclusive private school.

The hallways in the high school are narrow, and rooms are small; students hang their wraps on hooks at the entrance hall. The study hall-lunchroom is the church basement. The high school of 125 full-time students and 10 full-time teachers meets in the Sunday School designed for 200. Last year, 25 graduated from the Brethren Christian Schools. Thirteen went to college. According to reports, students compare favorably with neighboring public schools on achievement tests.

Penn High School and Paul Schmucker Middle School, located a few miles away, are ultramodern monuments to public school technology. The observer wonders why students would boycott such modern facilities for education in marginal surroundings. The students of the Christian high school don't appear rebellious because parents have put them there, nor do they seem to miss the large, impersonal high school.

David Miller, the young administrator, indicates that a Christian school is not just high school with Bible. Three elements make it Christian. (1) The teachers must be born again, having a Christian philosophy of education. The teacher still is the greatest influence on the pupil.

(2) All subject matter must be integrated with the Word of God. No truth is complete until every subject is interpreted in light of God's truth. (3) The Christian school must recognize the sinful nature of the pupil, realizing regeneration is necessary for learning Christian truth. Miller maintains it is impossible for students to learn without the divine enablement of conversion.

"A Christian school serves Christians. It is not a reformatory or remedial center," testifies Miller. The school will not receive students expelled from a public school unless there has been a time lapse where the enrolling student demonstrates personal responsibility. Even though the school is not an evangelistic arm of the community, two students accepted the Lord last year.

Miller indicates five avenues inculcate Christian character. (1) The school has a dress code that expresses Christian standards. The school does not use demerits to enforce discipline. Miller counsels with students and indicates, "If I have to talk five times with any one student, he is asked to leave." (None were asked to leave last year although three students withdrew because their attitudes were not harmonious with Christian education.) (2) The students are asked to sign a pledge that they will refrain from alcohol, tobacco, and drugs. (The students are not asked to refrain from dancing, movies, or other Christian taboos.) (3) Character education is reinforced by outward discipline. Miller used punctuality and attendance as illustrations. Three tardies become an absence, and students are asked to withdraw after 20 absences. (4) Academic averages are enforced. Those participating in student council, athletics, and other student committees must carry a "C" average. Students who transfer from public schools indicate grading is strict, and "A's" are hard to get. (5) Miller believes a Christian school must emphasize patriotism. In the past the school has not felt a need to "wave the flag" because of the conservative nature of the community; however, teaching patriotism is becoming more necessary, even in the small towns of conservative central Indiana. The pledge to the flag is said daily. Patriotic hymns are sung. Each day in chapel occurrences in history are noted. Students participate in "The Voice of Democracy" speech contest.

Out of the 21 members of the school staff, only 7 are members of Bethel Brethren Church and less than 13 percent of the pupils come from the church. The student body is drawn from 80 churches in the area. Yet, each member of the Board of Directors must be a member of Bethel Brethren Church. The church donates the facilities where the high school meets. The new modern elementary building and gym, along with the 20 acres valued at $250,000, is owned by the Brethren Christian School.

Local Church Sponsored Schools

In recent years, schools have been expanding among local churches. Whereas the parochial school provided education for a church's clientele, a local church sponsored school provides Christian education for all who want its advantages. Some Lutheran schools provide tuition free education for members (a registration fee is charged), but Christian schools in local churches usually provide school to all at the same fee. They believe education of the young is their responsibility (Matthew 28:20). Therefore, instead of teaching only on Sunday, school is also held Monday through Friday; sharing classrooms, gyms, cafeterias, playgrounds, chapels, libraries and visuals. They usually have broad Christian aims similar to interdenominational Christian schools. But the board of directors usually is drawn from the supporting church, and the capital assets belong to the congregation. Local church sponsored schools are found among Presbyterian, Baptist, Nazarene, Assembly of God, and a number of other denominations. The total number of schools in this group is unknown, and the number reported by the Department of Health, Education and Welfare is only the tip of the iceberg.

A New School in a Young Church

The Tri-City Christian Academy was conceived and founded by the pastor and less than 200 attenders of the Tri-City Baptist Church, Tempe, Arizona. The school began in September 1971, with 78 students, four teachers, a newly constructed school building, and an operating budget of $35,000 for that first year.

Leaving the security of a large Baptist church in Michigan, Pastor James Singleton began an independent church with two families in Tempe, Arizona, August 1969, meeting in a public school building, the Meyer Elementary School. Some might think a Christian school could not get momentum in a conservative suburban community, especially where busing was not an issue. There is less violence, less drug traffic, and a high standard of education in Tempe; nevertheless, Pastor James Singleton and the congregation founded the Christian Academy out of deep Christian motivations, both positive and negative in their urges.

The infant congregation had purchased 6.9 acres for $78,000 and, in April 1972, began selling bonds to construct their first permanent building. Singleton had struggled with the desire to minister to all the needs of his people, especially in regards to Christian education. While shaving one morning, he announced to his wife, "I believe the Lord wants us to start an academy . . . this fall." As he shared his vision with his 200 parishioners, he also enumerated the insurmountable obstacles: i.e., selling bonds for finances, constructing a building in four months, setting up a curriculum, determining policies, hiring teachers, and recruiting pupils. Since the church was founded on a pioneering spirit, the people approved their pastor's vision and began making preparations for the Tri-City Christian Academy, planning to open five months later with two grades. Singleton testifies, "The aim is not evangelism of children, even though the school has brought 10 or 12 families into the church. Our school has the positive aim to prepare Christian leadership which is the outstanding contribution a church can make to society." The more he talked of the academy, the more excited his members and neighbors became.

"Why not expand it to the third grade?" asked several parents who had eight-year-olds going into the third year of school.

"If we add the third grade . . . why not the fourth grade?" Someone suggested putting the two grades together in an old-fashioned schoolroom.

"Some called me crazy," the pastor replied, but the original registration of 12 students stretched to 78, and they began with grades one through eight the first year.

The mechanics were simple: one teacher taught two grades; a total of four teachers instructed the eight grades.

Some wanted a local board of parents to control the school, making the pastor an ex-officio board member. These argued that board of education members should be

educators who could give stability to the school. Singleton countered, "The academy will be controlled by the
local church, and the deacons will be its board members." He was not opposed to educators on the board, but
wanted a biblical philosophy at its core. The congregation
voted to keep spiritual principles at the core of the school
and, since that day, has supplied the necessary funds for
capitalization, equipment, and schoolbooks, and has made
up any deficit financing of the Tri-City Christian School.
The school is parochial in the true sense of the word.

Recently a letter from the State Superintendent of
Public Instruction asked the acedemy to fill out an extensive report. When Singleton viewed the form, it not
only requested the number of students in each grade, but
irrelevant and trivial information. Phoning the State
Department of Education, Singleton was told the superintendent was required to report to the legislature the
number of students in nonpublic schools, so that if private
schools were closed, they would know how many students
would be dumped into public schools. Singleton asked,
"Does the law require that I report to the Superintendent
of Public Instruction?" "No!" was the answer. Therefore,
Singleton instructed his principal to supply only the number of students in each grade. Before signing the question-
naire he wrote a disclaimer, "This report is voluntary and
the fact that I have returned it does not set a precedent
for succeeding years." In the ensuing two years, the academy did not file a report.

Singleton testified that the academy has higher academic standards than the public schools, pointing out
that, using identical tests, children from the academy rate
an average of two years higher than those in public
schools of Arizona. Also, he noted that, during each suc-

ceeding year, enrollment has gone up, rather than decreased. "The public buys a good product."

Singleton predicts enrollment will double again next
year. "The academy took two years to gain the confidence
of the public." Then, pointing to the expansion in the
lower grades: "These students will stay with us and provide a basis for adding more classes at the lower level, as
well as extending the academy to grade 12."

The academy has traditional discipline standards for its
students with a dress code (girls may not wear slacks but
modest dresses), and young boys must have short hair-
cuts.

Discipline is an integral part of education. First a *positive* slant is taken to help students self-direct their free
time in study hall, table work, and deportment. Also *negative* discipline is applied, so that misbehaving students
are suspended or detained, and some have even been
spanked. A few parents were quick to phone Pastor Singleton after their child was disciplined, one parent demanding, "Fire the teacher!" The strength of the academy
was reflected in Singleton's commitment to the printed
standards. Singleton backed up his principal and referred
all matters to the man the board had appointed over the
school. "The public found I wouldn't go over the head of
my principal and fire teachers at the whim of parents,"
Singleton testified. "Instead of losing students, we gained
the community's respect."

"We're not fighting the public school but promoting
quality education." Singleton is not known as a fighter
but as a church builder. But there is no positive action
without a counter reaction. Seeing the need of Christian
education to preserve the future of the church and the
nation, he preached six Sunday evening messages, "They

Are After Your Child." He named six influences that will destroy children: new education, drugs, sensitivity training, sex education, radical movements, and rock music.

In the past three years the church has constructed four buildings and the academy has grown from 78 students, operating this year on a budget of $125,000. The church supplies the necessary facilities, and the school purchases equipment and educational materials and pays salaries. All teachers have state college degrees and more than adequately meet the state requirements for certification.

Overnight Greatness

Singleton started small and attempted to build quality education slowly. Other Christian schools exploded overnight, riding the crest of opposition to forced busing, such as University Christian Schools in Jacksonville, Florida. The movement began in the fall of 1964 with seven students in kindergarten. Six years later they expanded to the first six grades and opened classes with 160 students, serving the families of the church that averaged 800 in attendance.

Forced crosstown busing for integration became an issue during 1970 and Jack Dinsbeer, the church's pastor, knew he had to expand the church's school. He knew parents would inundate the school the following fall. Beginning in April 1971, he borrowed $800,000 and built an educational plant for both Sunday School and University Christian School to accommodate 700 day school pupils. His move was both courageous and visionary, for if the forced busing was cancelled there was no way his church could pay off the indebtedness.

When the first building was under construction, Dinsbeer exercised super-faith and borrowed another $800,000 and began work on a second building, using plans identical to the first building.

Growth was so explosive that registration tables in the lobbies sometimes had as many as 100 parents waiting in line. It took several days to count the money, assign classes and organize the school for normal operation. Beginning with 1,860 students was a phenomenal success for Christian education, but a nightmare for school administrators.

The pastor stated that University Christian Schools is an evangelistic arm of the church; one of its goals is to reach unsaved students with the gospel. During a recent evangelistic crusade, the day-school bus routes were run each evening and a total of 415 students made decisions for Christ.

Problems Produced

The explosive growth produced problems. All of the teachers were Christians, but not all had a Christian philosophy of education, some bringing humanism from their public school experiences. Other teachers were Bible college graduates without certification or experience. Only 12 percent of the pupils came from the church, the others from the outside; most came because parents wanted to avoid sending their kids to inner-city schools.[4] As anyone knows, non-Christian kids don't act Christian. The administration was faced with the insurmountable problem of making a Christian school out of a "mixed multitude."

At first the school was criticized for lax standards. Pastor Dinsbeer took a significant role in the school that year. "We had hundreds of unsaved students and it took time to educate them to rules. I want a student to understand a rule he must obey." Although a few were expelled, Dins-beer is pleased with the large number of students who responded to Christian love and discipline.

University Christian School stands as a testimony that a private school can go first-class. The modern facilities located on 20 acres at University Boulevard and I-95 is as modern as any public school, with gymnasium, reading lab, biology lab, home economics rooms, typing rooms, and weight-lifting rooms.

A Honeywell computer records the grades, bills ac-counts, schedules events and keeps the many statistics needed in a large operation. The church's fleet of 35 buses transports students from all sections of Jacksonville. The print shop serving both school and church is as modern and complete as any in town.

We Don't Let Our Enemy Train Our Troops

At the other end of the spectrum and on the other side of the country is the Tabernacle Baptist School in Con-cord, California. There was no forced busing to propel this school into existence. But there were other problems. Con-cord is a suburb of San Francisco. Pastor Tom Bridges complains that the undisciplined graduates of Berkeley University have infiltrated the public schools of the area.

Rather than starting a large school and attempting to saturate the entire community, the pastor of Tabernacle Baptist Church purposely began small, with a view of creating a Christian nucleus of students, slowly building quality into a school to accomplish a Christian objective in the lives of those who came.

Beginning in 1971 with five kindergarten students, the effort may have been viewed as painfully anemic. In the second year the first two grades were added, with a total student body of 30 students; in 1973 there were 75 students enrolled in four grades. The school plans to add two grades each successive year. To understand the school's strategy is to analyze the pastor's motives for founding the school.

"I founded the school for three reasons: (1) the breakdown of morality in the public schools, (2) the deterioration of education in public schools because they have forsaken the fundamentals, and (3) to inculcate spiritual principles in the children of my church."

When faced with the criticism of "putting his kids in a hothouse," Bridges replied, "The charge is ridiculous. We don't turn our children over to the enemy to train them . . . we are preparing them to live the rest of their life." He points out that the greatness of a school is not its process but the end product, the pupil which it graduates. Then happily he points out that the students in Tabernacle Baptist Schools score one and one-half years above the public schools in the area, using the same standardized test. Bridges is deeply committed to a Christian culture in which to train pupils, noting that church and school complement each other in carrying out spiritual directives. He is angered by the "hothouse argument," noting public schools are not neutral as they once were: "They destroy lives." Also, Bridges points out that the hothouse argument has little validity; children are in school only 6 out of 24 hours a day and 5 out of 7 days a week. They are exposed to the world through television, shopping centers, playgrounds, and a multitude of other ways.

When the Tabernacle Baptist Schools was founded, there was not an immediate push to get children out of the public schools, since five Christian schools were within a radius of 15 miles from the church. The Bridges children were already enrolled in the Walnut Creek (California) Christian Schools. In counselling with several educators in the California Association of Christian Schools, he was advised to start slowly, build surely, and within a decade he would have a powerful institution. Bridges testifies that if they had started with students from all twelve grades the first year, the school would have had insurmountable problems in keeping a Christian environment. Public school pupils would have brought their problems and public school orientation with them. "Rather than a Christian school, I would have had a reformatory, trying to overcome the incipient failures of the public school," the patient pastor noted. "We couldn't have taught them." By starting small the teachers were able to establish a Christian culture and as other pupils were enrolled, they could be absorbed without wrecking the Christian environment in the school. Then Bridges commented, "We couldn't have taught in a disruptive environment." With assurance that he did the right thing, Tom Bridges commented, "We haven't had any problems to speak of and our Christian school has been a joy to administer." Now he smiles. "Just think of it . . . our children will never be exposed to the filth of the public schools!"

One impetus for the Tabernacle Christian School came when a church member, Harley Sly, also a teacher at the Concord High School, walked across the school lawn and saw his daughter sitting under a tree. Knowing she was cutting a class, he sent her back inside. Later that period he saw his daughter back under the tree again. She claimed the teacher didn't care if she came outside to read. This time taking her to the class, Sly demanded as a parent to know why the teacher was not properly instructing the class. The teacher swore at Sly, telling him it was none of his business what went on in the classroom. Sly was floored when the administration gave no help. He went to his pastor, despairing, "What can we do?"

"The Christian school is the only answer for our children!" Sly has publicly testified before the church. He also complains about lax morals, filthy language, and decaying standards at Concord High School; his fellow teachers treat him as a doomsday prophet.

A School Founded Out of Protest

Whereas the Concord School was a silent protest to the public schools, the Middletown Christian School grew out of a vocal attempt to make the public schools of Middletown, Ohio, serve the entire community rather than maintain a bias against Christianity. As youth pastor, Joe Lewis counseled with the 250 young people in the Grace Baptist Church of Middletown. He faced their problems: narcotics, vulgar language, pre-marital sex, violence, and anti-American feelings throughout the school. Also, evolution was taught with an anti-Christian bias. Lewis was appalled that his students were asked to read *Soul on Ice, Catcher in the Rye,* and other books he considered pornographic.

Lewis submitted the following survey to 229 junior and senior high students.

Yes   No

78% ____   1. Have you ever heard one of your school teachers use vulgar language in class?

40% ____   2. Have you ever heard a schoolteacher take the name of the Lord in vain in class?

55% ___ 3. Have you ever been approached by someone who wanted to sell or give you marijuana or any other narcotic?

45% ___ 4. Have any of your school friends used drugs?

35% ___ 5. Have you ever used drugs?

30% ___ 6. Do you know of any teacher who uses drugs?

90% ___ 7. Have you ever been taught evolution as a fact rather than a theory?

79% ___ 8. Have there ever been in your school any disturbances such as revolts, riots, student disorders, boycotts, etc.?

80% ___ 9. Have you ever heard the American way of life, the establishment, and capitalism criticized by a teacher?

70% ___ 10. Have you ever been taught that pre-marital sex is all right?

70% ___ 11. Have you been asked to read such books as *Of Mice and Men, Soul on Ice, The Grapes of Wrath, Catcher in the Rye,* or any other book that includes cursing?

40% ___ 12. Has the Bible ever been criticized by any of your teachers?

10% ___ 13. Has the Bible ever been praised or upheld by any of your teachers?

30% ___ 14. Has the Grace Baptist Church or any other fundamental church been openly criticized or ridiculed?

50% ___ 15. Has your own Christian witness been attacked, ridiculed or prohibited?

Armed with statistics, Lewis appeared before the Board of Education in Middletown, reading a petition respectfully requesting 11 changes in the public school. Vice President of the Board William Schaefer dealt with the explosive matter in patience and tact. Lewis did not ask for sectarian Christianity to be taught in the schools. He asked that in the teachers of Science courses be instructed to teach evolution as a theory, not a fact; that consideration be given to changing biology textbooks to include all theories of creation similar to a law recently enacted in California; that teachers not be allowed to use vulgar language or cursing; that teachers not be allowed to ridicule or condemn the American system; that any teaching on sex education not encourage but rather discourage premarital sex. Reading from a prepared manuscript, Lewis stated, "We strongly recommend that students who are so rebellious that they are disrupting the learning process in our school system be denied further access to the privilege of free public education. We recommend as necessary that tax dollars be used for court action to obtain the right to expel any rebellious students."

Like throwing an egg into the fan, the local newspaper erupted during following weeks with agitation on both sides of the issue. One letter to the editor received headline treatment, charging that Lewis's "tactics are similar to Hitler's." The Board of Directors wrote a letter to Lewis, indicatin⌐   had made charges without substantiation; they requested that students submit the names of teachers guilty of such infractions.

Lewis announced to the newspapers that he would supply his students with forms to report to the School Board delinquencies by teachers. Mrs. Joan Compton, member of the Board of Education, warned that students who planned to make written reports of their teachers should be aware of legal implications. The newspaper stated, "Mrs. Joan Compton . . . warned that any signed statements could result in lawsuits by teachers mentioned in reports." Letters to the editor in the newspaper continued the ferment.

The Newsline, the local house organ of Middletown Teachers Association, a branch of the Ohio Education Association, took a survey of its own. According to the Middletown *Journal, The Newsline* went after several people and situations with a sarcastic flare, but, most notably, it took a few pokes at the Grace Baptist Church's survey of its teenage congregation. *The Newsline* reported that, "86 percent of the students thought that marijuana was the capital of Mexico, 100 percent of the students said they would steal from the church collection plate if they thought they could get away with it, and 96 percent of the students thought that the Last Supper was Friday's meal in the school cafeteria." When students in public schools were asked about the survey, none remembered it. Someone accused it of the public schools bias against Christianity.

Getting no satisfaction from the Board of Directors, the Grace Baptist Church announced the founding of its school in the spring of 1972. First it issued a printed statement, "Why Christian Schools?" giving three primary reasons for founding the Middletown Christian School: (1) Religious Reasons—The Bible commanded parents to teach their children all of the time (Deut. 6:4–9), that the blessing of God would follow those who obey the instruction of children. (2) Philosophical Reasons—The brochure stated God is the center of life and is the Maker of the universe. Stating, "We want to pass along this philosophy to our children . . . we need a school that is based on God's Word." Noting that, "Our children are

God's children," the statement indicated a Christian school is the only expression of this philosophy. (3) Practical Reasons—The statement did not condemn the public schools for their negative influence but noted that a Christian environment was different from a secular environment, even if the secular environment were moral and upright. The church came to the conclusion that its children would have to be educated in a Christian environment if they were going to be Christian.

Next, the founders of Middletown Christian School wrote out a statement of purpose and objectives. The purpose of the school was: (1) To establish Christian truth as a guide for life, (2) to maintain a high academic standard, (3) to instill pure morals in the heart of pupils, (4) to generate a spirit of patriotism, and (5) to live a disciplined life. Each of these statements had a number of sub-points, reflecting the extent of thought that went into Middletown Christian Schools.

In the fall of 1972, the school opened with kindergarten through grade 12, meeting in the old facilities of Grace Baptist Church. There were seven teachers that first year. Ron Miller and Earl Spenser graduated from high school at the end of the first year. The curriculum was designed by Accelerated Christian Education, basically a programmed education approach to learning. There were only 22 students in the high school that first year.

During the school year the church moved to a new million-dollar facility situated on 34 acres, located on I-75, giving room for future expansion; 370 students enrolled for the second year. The students are energetic and infectious in their support of the school, even though they realize they have sacrificed some of the material advantages of a secular high school.

Begun on Christian principles, this is not a "backlash" school against integration, as there are blacks in the school. The Middletown Christian School is unashamedly committed to fundamental Christianity. However, it is not an evangelistic effort to get people saved. Joe Lewis says we are attempting to carry out the Great Commission, "Teaching them to observe all things whatsoever I have commanded you" (Matt. 28:20).[5]

Busing in Reverse

One of the largest buildings in Somonauk, Illinois, (population 800) is the Somonauk Christian Schools located in the Somonauk Baptist Temple. No one in his wildest imagination would have believed a large church or school could be built on the flat cornfields of Central Illinois, but the church attendance last spring averaged over 600. A massive two-story $550,000 brick and steel structure stands as a sentinel watching over the snow-covered winter fields. Almost 200 students inside receive an old-fashioned American education. The church has an extensive evangelistic ministry to 20 surrounding smaller towns without churches, busing children to Somonauk for Sunday School. Many are bused to the Christian School during the week, comprising what one report called "busing that reverses the trend of our day."

Pastor Russell Keller has had a running battle with the public schools in Somonauk, complaining to the School Board that one teacher smokes pot, has had an abortion, and advocates free love. The students from the church came to Keller complaining to him about her influence on other students. First, Keller went and spoke to her and her husband in the home, explaining the conservative stand of the church. Next he went to the School Board but received little encouragement with his endeavors to thwart her influence. This began his consideration of starting the Christian schools.

The church sponsored a youth evangelistic meeting with a speaker who directed a drug recovery home in Houston, Texas. The speaker was scheduled to address an assembly in the local high school. Certain elements in the school community protested because the evangelist was holding meetings at Somonauk Baptist Temple, and the principal cancelled the assembly because of the pressure, telling Keller, "I want to keep peace in the school." Keller told a large rally at the County Fair to "Go home and phone the principal to protest the cancelling of the assembly." The school official was deluged with calls; many residents came by his house to register their complaints. At 2:00 a.m., the principal yielded and rescheduled the speaker for an assembly.

When Keller found out that there was not an American flag in each of the rooms at the public school, he announced the fact from the pulpit and told his people to stand for patriotism. The school superintendent called Keller the following morning and accused him of stirring up trouble in the community. "I'm not stirring up trouble; I'm pointing out that we don't have American flags in our public school rooms," responded Keller. He went on to say, "I love our schools and want to see them patriotic." Today there is a flag in each room of the public school.

Keller complained to the school officials about the dirty halls, dirty bulletin boards, profanity on the bathroom walls, and children attending school dressed any way they pleased. Keller expressed his educational philosophy: "When pupils lounge around, doing what they want to, dressed any way they please, they have no respect for authority." Keller observes, "I like to see chairs in a straight row, to show that education is disciplined and leads to a controlled life."

The pastor first hired Brian Mayfield, Principal, in January 1973, and together they began to plan for the Somonauk Christian Schools. No teacher was hired without three interviews: Mayfield evaluated their academic background, Keller evaluated their spiritual background, and together they closely scrutinized every aspect of the teacher's life. Keller shocked the applicants by asking, "Do you have any homosexual problems?" The leaders are careful about character and conduct. He told the men teachers they can't touch the girls; the single teachers must be careful in their dating life.

Out of Deep Conviction

The school was founded out of deep conviction; the congregation was willing to pay the price because of their desire to provide the type of education not found in public schools. Nine full-time teachers were hired and a curriculum planned for 300 students, with an operating budget of $257,000 in the first year. The church constructed a $550,000 dual-purpose building with air conditioning, carpeted, full-size gym with showers, lockers and modern equipment. Keller believes that "a church should put its pocketbook where its mouth is, when it comes to convictions."

Mayfield points out that the public school is pupil-centered, noting this is an unchristian emphasis. "Our school will be teacher-centered; pupils must learn respect for authority." But Mayfield was quick to point out "A Christian school must be balanced, reflecting the truth as found in the Bible. It not only is teacher-centered but must be life-oriented and curriculum-based." He noted that the greatest teacher of all, Jesus Christ, was teacher-centered in His classrooms."

"We will not teach the new math," indicated Pastor Keller. He refers to a *Wall Street Journal* article reporting that students' test scores went down because of the new math. He explained that new math was developed to cause pupils to understand the meaning behind mathematics. But proper understanding didn't always lead to proper performance, just as correct understanding of the Scripture does not necessarily produce correct life. "We will have old-fashioned classes with memory work, homework and arithmetic flashcards." Keller explained that when children were conditioned through correct practice, they could add, subtract, and multiply.

When Keller attempts to create a Christian environment for his school he wants it to be *positive*, to reinforce correct living, but also *negative* to condition students against filth. "I want the young people in my church to be sensitive against sin . . . I do want them in a Christian hothouse environment." Because of this, Keller will enforce a dress code and conduct code. "A hothouse will build character in them, not weaken them." He states, "Children become like those who influence them most, and I want them repulsed by sin." He illustrates: "If you stick a man head-first into a garbage can he will fight it and be incensed. I want my young people to be incensed by sin and fight it." Keller points out that children who live around sin become adjusted to it—used to it; he maintains that public school education teaches kids to adjust to sin.

When someone accuses Keller of brainwashing his children, he replies, "It's our church's responsibility to do everything possible, even brainwashing, to get our children to live like the people of the Bible." He goes on to explain, "I will beg, bribe, prod, even brainwash, to get them to do what God requires." Keller quickly explains that the term *brainwashing* must be defined as simply "directing the students toward the truth that is in Jesus Christ." Keller accuses the public school of brainwashing; i.e., directing children toward their concept of truth, but "they are wrong." Therefore, Keller concludes "We must do everything within our power to direct our children towards the truths found in the Word of God."

CONCLUSION

The cacophony of voices criticizing the public schools carries little weight in the minds of listeners. No matter how desperate a situation, the American public seldom heeds a complaint against its sacred institutions until the criticism is given time to fester. Only when a single voice of opposition swells to choral proportion will the American public rise in indignation to demand changes. The public schools are in trouble, and there is no light at the end of the tunnel. Crime, violence, and declining standards have done nothing to enhance the public's enchantment with their local school. Perhaps the rise of the private schools will target in on the Achilles' heel of public school. Private schools operate in cleanliness, order, and determination. Almost without exception, they present documents proving their children outscore those from public school. Perhaps their quality will expose the deteriorative condition of public schools. Perhaps the increasing numbers of private schools can give credence to the varied voices criticizing public schools. The private school is more than vocal philosophical dissent; it involves tuition, building, uniforms, fees, and textbooks—hard cash on the line. The private school is a protest come of age.

For many years, churches allowed the public schools to communicate both character and education; congregations held the right to instruct their young in Bible content on Sunday morning. But that nonverbalized agreement has broken down. One pastor noted, "We're not deserting the public schools; they have abandoned us." As a result, thousands of churches are moving into the education business. What began as a vocal protest has grown to a militant tide. Churches will not sit idly by and see the public school desecrate their young.

When it comes to the opportunity of educating the Christian youth of America, *the public school has had it* and has blown it. The Christian schools are a protest come of age.

NOTES

1. Martin Essenburg would like to emphasize the following: "It is not the *Church* that educates, but rather *parents*. It is not the Church that has 294 schools, but rather the NUCS."

2. The others come from a variety of churches and from homes desiring a Christian school.

3. The regulations of the schools thus reflect parental opinions, and there does not seem to be much tension on these points. However, the school does enforce a few simple regulations, such as not permitting blue jeans. Parents readily support this.

4. Where quality education was lacking.

5. The curriculum was designed by the faculty and staff to meet the minimum standards of Ohio, but also to incorporate Bible and other related Christian subjects. It is a mission work as well as a place of academic excellence, for over 60 students were saved in the year of this report.

4 How Fast Are They Growing?

The public school enterprise is one of the largest businesses in the United States, occupying the attention of 62.8 million people, annually spending over $90 billion, meeting in over 130,000 school building located on an unknown amount of acreage called playgrounds and public property.[1] Some feel that the only larger landholder in the United States is the Federal Government.

Last year 59.5 million students enrolled in our public schools; they were instructed by three million teachers, and supervised by about 300,000 superintendents, principals and other instructional staff members. Out of a nation of 209 million people, about three out of every ten persons were directly involved in the American educational process.[2]

About three million persons graduated from high school, representing 76 percent of those who began school in 1959. This means three out of every four children who began first grade graduated from high school. Of the graduates, 47 percent entered a degree program in a college or university. Twenty-four percent of our high school graduates will earn a bachelors degree, eight percent a masters degree, and 1.5 percent a doctorate degree.[3]

America is spending more money on its pupils than ever before. Ten years ago (1961–62) an estimated

$419.00 was spent on each pupil. The total invested in each pupil more than doubled this past year to $934.00 in 1971–72. The biggest item in the school budget is teachers' salaries; the average teacher received $10,140. Ten years ago there were 25.7 pupils per teacher, whereas last year there were 22 pupils for each self-contained classroom. Ten years ago 15 percent of the teachers did not have a bachelors degree, as compared with 1971–72, when only 3 percent did not hold the minimum require-

They Have the Best

ments of a college degree.[1]

The public schools should be doing a better job than at any time in the history of the United States. They are spending more money on each pupil by teachers who have better educations, smaller classes and more time. Just about everything the public schools have requested, they have received.

The public schools have better of everything at least they claim superiority to private schools. They have multicolor, age-graded testbooks relevant to the needs of contemporary students. Curriculums have been prepared for the emerging generation, with new math and new English, giving the students a new curriculum.

The public schools have educational TV films, overhead projectors, slides, tape players, record players; they have access to every educational advantage that plugs into the wall. They have spacious air conditioned buildings with carpeted halls, gyms, athletic fields, locker rooms, swimming pools, handball courts, paved courses for driver education, and libraries loaded with books.

The public schools take advantage of what they think is the best educational groupings, scheduling with team teaching, small groupings, modular schedulings, group counselings, community relations committees and individualized instruction in learning labs.

The public schools maintain they have discovered the ultimate in socialization; they have motivational psychology, they have guidance counselors, and students are realizing self-actualization. No longer is there an identity crisis.

The public schools claim they have better administration through job description, organizational charts, management techniques, delegation of responsibility and appropriate accountability.

The schools have consolidated to offer better opportunities; they have bused to overcome social evils; they have broadened education to prepare for jobs, enrich recreational life, humanize insensitive pupils, find lost identity and produce proper mental health.

Yet, with more and more of everything better and better, Johnny still can't read. He might be beaten up in the restrooms, offered a joint, learn profanity, sneer at the principal, or do anything else he jolly well pleases. He won't do as well on the college boards nor learn reverence for his country.

Private Schools

As a result, Americans are turning to private schools for various reasons. For the most part, the private school is an unknown factor to average Americans. About all they know is that the largest Catholic church in the area usually has a parochial school, usually on church property.

One out of every ten pupils in America attends a private school; the average is probably much higher if actual statistics could be gathered. There are 16,453 nonpublic schools operating with 5,143,182 pupils and 216,825 teachers.[5] The total number of Roman Catholic schools is dropping, while that of nonreligious and religious private schools is increasing rapidly. The National Center for Educational Statistics reports, "There was an over-all 10 percent drop in enrollments in nonpublic schools during the past decade." [6] The Roman Catholic schools lost 19.3 percent of their enrollment over the last ten years. At the same time, nonreligious private schools demonstrated a growth in enrollment of 90.8 percent. This startling growth shows Americans are turning to private schools. While the Roman Catholics were declining, Protestant religious schools reported a 47.0 percent increase. [7]

The reported overall number of nonpublic schools has remained about the same; nevertheless the growth of Christian and nonreligious private schools in the past few years should be predictive of continued expansion in the future. The movement is experiencing growth. Al Janney, of the American Association of Christian Schools, indicates new schools are opening at the rate of 100 a month. As private schools increase, public school educators will become increasingly defensive. As more and more parents turn to private schools, a growing repudiation of tax-supported schools is revealed.

The South Loses

The South is the only section of the country to show a decrease in public schools. They lost 6.1 percent in elementary and secondary schools in 1970-71.

However, statistics concerning the Christian schools released by the National Center for Educational Statistics are not complete. They list only two Baptist private schools in the state of Georgia, while the yellow pages in the Savannah phone directory list five Baptist schools. The National Center lists 172 Baptist schools in the entire nation, whereas Janney indicates there are probably 400 Baptist schools in the state of Florida alone. He estimates from his observation that there are 3,000 Fundamentalist churches operating a school including anywhere from only kindergarten to many which offer kindergarten through grade 12. As a reflection of the growth on strength of Christian schools in local churches, last October 1973, a meeting to constitute the Eastern Christian Education Association was held at the Statler Hilton, Washington, D.C. They expected 500 delegates from Christian schools to attend, over 800 were present.

Discrepancies in released statistics of (HEW) arise from four possible causes. First, many private schools in conservative churches will not report their statistics to any federal agency. They begin a school system in opposition to the public school and feel that filing a report is the first step toward governmental control. James Singleton, pastor, Tri-City Baptist Church where the Tri-City Christian Academy is located, would not file a statistical report with the state of Arizona, claiming, "The more they know about us, the more they want to control our program." Joe Lewis, principal at Middletown (Ohio) Christian Academy, states, "We started our school because of the failure of the public school; they will try to regulate our program and cause us to fail as they have failed."

A second reason for the missing statistics; there is no national organization to compile a mailing list or membership roll. The very fact that many Christian schools are independent indicates they will not affiliate with any organization, even to being listed on the roll of an educational association. Therefore, the National Center for Educational Statistics has an impossible task in attempting to list all private schools.

A third reason for the missing statistics comes from a

procedural misjudgment by the National Center for Educational Statistics. They admitted, "The low response rates among non-Catholic schools made it necessary to select a subsample of the nonresponding non-Catholic schools for a special follow-up effort. The resulting sample data was used to inflate the national and regional totals for this missing segment of schools." [8] The technique is programmed for failure. If they take a smaller section and project it on the national basis, their final figure would be inaccurate because they began with an incomplete figure in the sectional list.

The following profile of a private school will illustrate the typical nonpublic school. The average private school has 292.3 pupils and approximately 12 teachers in each school. Whereas the public schools have 22 pupils per teacher, the private schools show an average of 26.9 per teacher. However, the secondary school ratio was healthier, with 17.3 pupils per high school teacher. The number of small private schools is decreasing, while the number of large schools is growing. This does not mean that small schools are going out of existence; rather, it means that more pupils are being enrolled in smaller schools, hence they are climbing to a higher bracket. [9]

Approximately one-third (31.9) of all private schools have opened their doors since 1954. [10] Many think the private schools are old-line academics for the blue blood, when in fact they comprise a young, vibrant, "grass roots" movement.

The 16,453 private schools in the U.S. are spread over the following distributions: (See Table A) [11]

The growth of non-Catholic schools is noteworthy. The statistics show that Roman Catholic schools decrease by 19.3 percent on a nationwide basis. But, buried away on

Table A.—Number and percent of nonpublic elementary and secondary schools, by region and affiliation: United States, 1970–71

Affiliation	Total U.S.	REGION								
		New England	Mideast	Great Lakes	Plains	South-east	South-west	Rocky Mountains	Far West
Total	16,453	1,347	4,221	3,976	1,685	2,355	771	322	1,776
Nonaffiliated	2,136	323	436	196	83	669	103	38	288
Affiliated	14,270	1,023	3,775	3,777	1,590	1,681	664	282	1,478
Baptist	172	1	15	11	0	63	9	3	70
Christian Reformed	146	0	5	63	33	12	3	3	27
Friends	44	5	31	2	1	2	0	1	2
Jewish	255	16	170	28	3	18	2	1	17
Lutheran	1,354	6	85	604	305	111	78	32	133
Methodist	63	0	6	1	1	42	6	0	7
Presbyterian	31	0	3	0	1	20	6	1	0
Episcopal	348	23	70	8	7	122	60	2	56
Roman Catholic	10,770	934	3,146	2,845	1,165	1,123	460	182	915
7th-day Adventist	658	34	80	130	49	114	13	42	196
Other affiliated	429	4	164	85	25	54	27	15	55
Unknown	47	1	10	3	12	5	4	2	10

page 27 of the report, figures reveal that nonaffiliated private schools increased by 90.9 percent on a nationwide basis. Growth of private schools in the South is greatest, a staggering 240 percent increase. Yet a large number of private schools in the South are missing from the survey, making the percentage actually much higher, a trend that should be noted by public school educators, lawmakers and parents.

Facing the Question

The question needs to be faced, "Why be concerned with missing statistics about private Christian schools?" First, boards of education make policy based on statistics, such as those found in the report. If they have dismissed the private school movement from their thinking, perhaps its size should demand some attention. Boards of education should ask the question, "What is lacking in our program of studies that cause parents to invest in the added cost of private education?" This question, honestly faced by public school educators, should provoke changes.

When lawmakers vote extra funds for public schools, they base their funding on the size of the public school and the efficiency they assume exists in their programs. If lawmakers knew the size of the private school movement, they might question the present use of funds and examine new appropriations much more carefully.

Finally, faulty statistics keep the American public in the dark regarding the size of the private school movement. If enough parents knew the size of the movement, they could band together to make changes in the public schools. However, parents "struggle alone," feeling it is hopeless to voice an opinion against such a giant as the public schools of America.

The private Christian school is a return of rugged individualism like their Puritan forefathers, modern-day
parents pay the price for their children's future. With
ideals displayed like banners in the wind, some Christian
schools meet in Sunday School buildings, while others
meet in modern brick-and-steel facilities. Some pupils
walk on raw cement floors, a thick coat of paint covers
concrete block walls. While some use the *McGuffey
Reader,* others used programmed education for children
in individualized learning labs. These private Christian
schools discredit the assumption that more tax money will
produce better education.

In spite of low budgets, both pupil and teacher reflect
high optimism. They have sacrificed the enrichment of
swimming pools and tackle football. They don't have the
computerized language lab nor the battery of counselors
to help pupils choose colleges. Sports are energetically
pursued, but most Christian schools couldn't beat the
public high school down the street. The hot lunches are
missing; so are the woodworking shops, mechanical draw-
ing rooms, drama theater, well-equipped science labs, and
an office full of clerks to keep records. But students get
a superior education; they memorize history because their
teachers believe students can't appreciate the future without insight into the past. Some wear uniforms, most keep
quiet in study hall, and all salute the flag. In a Christian
school, pupils are prayed over.

With faith and determination, educators from Christian schools march forth to teach, with better facilities
than Mark Hopkins, who only asked for a log. They educate, realizing the ultimate test of a school is not its
curriculum, textbooks, teachers or equipment. A school
is only as good as the pupil who emerges from the class-

room. They return to fundamentals, because the graduate is the length and shadow of a school.

NOTES

1. Kenneth A. Simon, W. Vance Grant, *Digest of Educational Statistics, 1972 Edition.* (Washington, D. C.: U. S. Department of Health, Education, and Welfare, National Center for Educational Statistics, U. S. Government Printing Office, 1973), p. 1. This volume represents the statistics used by government in dealing with educational matters.

2. *Ibid.*

3. *Ibid.,* p. 2.

4. *Ibid.,* p. 3-4.

5. Diane B. Gertler, *Statistics of Nonpublic Elementary and Secondary Schools, 1970-71.* (Washington, D. C.: U. S. Department of Health, Education, and Welfare, National Center for Educational Statistics, U. S. Government Printing Office, 1973), p. 3. This volume represents the statistics used by the government in dealing with private schools. In most areas they are complete and reliable, but many private Protestant schools (local church schools) will not return statistics, hence raising a question of the report's reliability concerning private Protestant schools.

6. *Ibid.*

7. *Ibid.,* p. 3-5.

8. *Ibid.,* p. 2.

9. *Ibid.,* p. 3-5.

10. *Ibid.*

11. *Ibid.,* p. 6.

5 The Public Schools Lash Out

Have you ever stood at a second story window and watched two shoppers, laden with packages, head for the same corner from different directions, to arrive simultaneously? The crash was inevitable. A growing host of Americans are no longer satisfied with the public school system. The Christian school is unique, it is not just a public school with Bible teaching. The public school and the Christian school are like duelers, lined up back to back, prepared to walk in opposite directions. However, their cross-purposes will ultimately clash.

Parents who have criticized the public schools apparently had little success. Now they are taking the final step—boycotting the public schools. The Christian school movement is a protest come of age. Like striking employees who withhold their work, parents are withholding their children. This "slap-in-the-face" is not sitting well with the public schools. The public schools are lashing out.

First, public school educations are mocking private schools. In an article in *The Atlanta Journal,* July 1, 1973, Lee County School Superintendent Robert A. Clay is quoted, "Segregation academics is really the only name you could give to any of the private schools in southwest Georgia." [1] Next, the *Savannah Morning News* reports that the blue ribbon MFPE Committee in its study of the school system in Georgia has recommended "that the state immediately require private elementary and secondary schools to meet the same minimum legal standards as public schools." [2]

Maryland recently raised the requirement for a chauffeur's license for those driving school buses. The restrictions made it impossible for the schools to get enough drivers for the beginning of the school year. A waiver exempted those driving for public schools. Reverend John Macon, President of Bible Baptist Schools, Clinton, Maryland, demanded licenses for his drivers, pounding on the counter, "We're Americans, too!"

Prince George County legislators were faced with a bill requiring private schools to construct a six-foot high fence and 10 feet of shrubbery, an ordinance suggested by the Parks and Planning Department.

"We're not Stalag 17," Macon told a state congressional committee. He pointed out insurance rates were lower on private schools than public schools because their students didn't tear up their school. "Private school buildings don't need to be protected from students." Then he asked, "Why do you require public schools to have a three-foot fence but ours is six-foot?"

But the grand finale came when Macon received a certified letter from the Division of Day Care in Prince George's County, Maryland, stating 18 items where his school was in violation. The letter read, "Four-year-olds were coerced by staff direction to try to read and to attempt other academic tasks . . . Four and five-year-olds had been coerced to memorize and chant in unison all of chapter 13 of 1 Corinthians from the Christian Bible." (April 4, 1973, signed.) The letter cites "Regulations, section 83" which prohibits injuring children's mental health. Does the Division of Child Day Care and Child Development in Maryland consider that teaching a four-year-old to read injures his mental health? Macon asked, "Is this a trend where social workers will accuse Christianity of being injurious to mental health?"

Macon told the press, "Religious freedom was born in Maryland because of the Catholic settlers. Let's not let it die here."

Macon got a court injunction prohibiting the agency from returning to his property without his permission or from interfering with his religious liberty.

The quiet disagreement between public schools and the church school is growing into a noisy revolution. Just as in a revolution, men fight for freedom. The church is leading a counterrevolution, attempting to bring itself back to the strength of God-centered education that originally built this nation. At present, the battle is fought in educational journals and pulpits. A few skirmishes are being held in state assemblies where laws are being passed opposing the Christian day school movement. Next, the battle will break out at the court level. The basic question is, "Who has the right to educate children?" The public schools claim they have responsibility for education of our nation's young. The church claims that God gave the responsibility of children to parents. This includes their education. The church claims that its mandate for family/church control of education is revealed from God in Holy Scripture. The public schools claim they must control education for the future of the republic. They follow the dictates of their sociological surveys and educational assumptions. As the battle grows greater, philosophical blood will be shed.

During the past decade, the battle has concerned itself within public schools. The question between public schools and churchmen has been, "What can be done with prayer, Bible reading, and religious exercises in the public school?" The Supreme Court did not rule out prayer; educational bureaucrats did. The supreme court did not rule out the Bible; educational administrators did. The public schools can sponsor a course on the history of Christianity or comparative religions. The Bible can be taught as literature. An objective analysis can be made in history courses on the contribution of Christianity to the United States. The church is largely unconscious of the things it can do to foster its influence in the public schools. The public has swallowed the lie that our schools cannot mention religion. Teachers are uninformed about the legal use of Bible and religion in their classrooms.

When a young girl passed out religious literature on the school bus (it was permitted away from school property), she was called into the principal's office and asked not to do so. "You'll make waves," the principal said. In the same school, pupils were allowed to wear black arm bands in sympathy with the bombing of Viet Nam during Christmas, 1972.

When it comes to religion, the public school still has a hot potato on its hands, no matter how many Christians enroll in a private school. The school that excludes Christianity is implying that it has been unimportant in the development of the United States, an inference not born out by facts. The public school claims they are neutral toward Christianity, but this is not the case. Christianity has been expelled from our public schools because of disagreement regarding its doctrine. If we excluded everything from school about which people disagree, the school would be completely sterile. But, if the public school taught Christianity, it would be in trouble. The courts have ruled correctly, that public schools may not indoctrinate its young in the Bible. They can not sponsor a revival meeting, a Mass, prayer groups, the Lord's table, or a Bar Mitzvah; schools can't even baptize. Because Christianity has been thrown out of the public schools, both education and our nation has suffered. The question still remains, "How can the Christian influence that has built our nation be experienced in our schools without doing violence to the Constitution that separates church and state?"

Written into our Constitution is the guarantee of religious liberty, stating that congress shall make no laws regarding religion. Separation of church and state is never disputed and is the basis of strength found in our churches when compared to state churches. This volume does not suggest that the public schools should teach religion nor does it suggest that either public schools or the church should oppose each other. On the contrary, the public schools should support our churches and the churches support the public schools. However, there is a growing rift between the two. There is a growing attack by the public schools on the church with its slams, slurs, questions, and outright mockery of the contribution of Christianity, much less its spiritual influence. As a result, the church has become defensive. Ministers have entered into arguments with the public schools. Today, the church is mounting a new offensive against the public schools, churches are building schools of their own.

Religion in the public schools is no longer the crucial debate, although it remains an issue.

Some Americans feel the critical question is, Should tax

money be used to support private schools? While this question is debated in Congress and various suits are filed with the Supreme Court, a deeper question is developing.

In the future, the new issue is the freedom of the Christian day school movement. The rapid growth of Christian schools is a threat to public schools. As the movement grows in quality and quantity, it indicts the public schools for their failure. Embarrassed public school educators cannot allow the Christian school movement to flourish. They instigate battles over zoning ordinances; local zoning boards say that Christian schools may not move into churches. The battle is enlarged by building inspectors, enforcing an unworkable code on Christian day schools. Still further, the battle is carried on by state boards of education issuing varying objections from state to state, that no one can teach unless: (1) the school is accredited; (2) the teachers are licensed; (3) the number of hours of Bible classes per week is controlled; (4) curriculum offerings are regulated by the state board of education. All these matters are questions of freedom. Can the Christian school teach what it feels is necessary for the pupil within its congregation?

The Public Schools Do Not Give Birth to Children—Parents Do

The public schools have not rested in their push for state control of education. Public schools have filed lawsuits contending that they are responsible for education, while courts have historically maintained it is the parents' responsibility. There is coming a crisis of ownership: Who owns our children?

The public school continues to invade the prerogatives of the home, assuming teachers can educate children better than parents can because they are professionals. Several court suits filed at the turn of the century were lost by the public schools; each time the parent retained the right to educate his child. However, in 1960 the State of Ohio passed a law that is yet to be contested in the courts, starting, "The natural rights of parents to custody and control of their children are subordinate to the power of the state to provide for the education of such infant children. Laws providing for the education of children are for the protection of the state itself" (Revised Education Code—1960, P. 195, Ohio School Guide. Section 7.06, "Compulsory Education Law").

America was not built by state-controlled individuals; as a matter of fact this is the type of government they fled in Europe. America was built and has risen as a world power through the freedom of the individual. The State of Ohio will lead the way in destroying that freedom. Compulsory attendance laws may become the Trojan Horse that tips our nation into godlessness. At present, every child of a specified age must attend school as defined by law. On the positive side, compulsory attendance laws have provided one of the highest literacy rates in the world and built strong individual freedom, contributing to a strong nation. However, with the deterioration of public school education (see Chapter two), parents should have the freedom to educate their children wherever they please. But the state has taken upon itself the responsibility of deciding what is and what is not a school. Implied in this question is the certification of teachers; with the passing of time, only those who have state certification may teach the children. In time, a person may be excluded from teaching in a Christian school or any school because they hold a biblical educational point of view. American freedom demands that parents decide who will educate their children, what constitutes a school, and what constitutes education.

God has given the responsibility of the child's education to parents: "Train up a child in the way he should go: And when he is old, he will not depart from it" (Prov. 22:6). The Hebrew family was given the *Shema*, their greatest commandment, "The Lord our God is one Lord: And thou shalt love the Lord thy God with all thine heart, and with all thy soul, and with all thy might" (Deut. 6:4-5). So important was this commandment that God said, "These words, which I command thee this day, shall be in thine heart: and thou shalt teach them diligently unto thy children, and shalt talk of them when thou sittest in thine house, and when thou walkest by the way, and when thou liest down, and when thou risest up" (Deut. 6:6-7). God prescribes this commandment to be kept before the eyes of the children and written on the doorpost of the house, lest they forget the Lord brought them out of the bondage of Egypt (Deut. 6:8-10). Obviously, education was the responsibility of parents, just as the New Testament commanded, "Children, obey your parents in the Lord" (Eph. 6:1) The fathers were commanded, "Bring them (children) up in the nurture and admonition of the Lord" (Eph. 6:4). Whether the parent did the actual instruction, or saw that the child went to the Temple where the Rabbi could teach them, education was still the parental responsibility. Parents paid their tithes to support the Levites, priests, and rabbis.

When a child did not obey, the parent was held responsible, as in the case of the death of the priest Eli. He was judged because he did not rear his children properly (1 Sam. 2:17; 4:17-18). When the nation Israel was taken into captivity God reminded them that the sins of the parents would be visited upon the children (Deut. 5:9).

Clearly, the Bible teaches that the basic responsibility for the training of children is with the parents, not the state. The state doesn't give birth to children; mothers and fathers have children.

Have the Public Schools Violated the Constitution?

One of the serious questions posed by this book has vast ramifications. Are the public schools standing in violation of the separation of church and state? The June, 1963, Supreme Court ruling declared mandatory public prayer and Bible reading in classrooms unconstitutional. This ruling should have made the public school amoral or areligious. Public schools have worked hard to rid themselves of the "Protestant's" God. Decades ago the Catholics recognized the "Protestant influence" in our public schools and founded a Catholic parochial school system to preserve their Catholic religious traditions. Now, Protestants are building schools to preserve their Protestant traditions.

The public schools have a singular adherence to secular humanism, defined as a total life-style without reference to or need of God. However, secular humanism is not amoral or areligious. Secular humanism is a religion, both by definition and court ruling. The courts have recognized secular humanism as a religion and California has passed laws that creationism should be taught as one of the options to the scientific explanation of our nation. Most Christians view this decision as a great victory because Creationism was required to be taught in the public schools, when in fact the greater triumph was recognition of secular humanism as a religion. The educational process should transmit knowledge, understanding and skills of our culture, completely apart from sectarian Christianity. But we have seen the state adopt secular humanism as its religion, where the state decides what is right and wrong, making a "god" out of the judgments of the state. Hence the public schools are pushing a godless religion while forcing out Christianity.

Secular humanism is also a religion by the definition of religion: "Religion is concerned with what exists beyond the visible world . . . operates through faith or intuition rather than reason . . . arises naturally out of an inner need." Most dictionaries do not include a Supreme Being in their definition of religion. Religions such as Buddhism, Taoism, and Bahaism center around a unique ethical culture, to the exclusion of deity. Therefore, communism or secular humanism are religions.

The National Association of Christian Schools states in a brochure that "Secular [humanism] education affirms its faith that in the beginning was chance, that man is an animal, that truth is relative, that history has no meaning, that life has no purpose, and that death is the end." These are the articles of faith of secular humanism. If the interpretation of Christianity cannot be given in a classroom, why can the religion of secular humanism be taught? This rhetorical question will not be answered. But every educational system has its assumed values growing out of the religion of the masses. Secular humanism is the current religion of the American masses and its doctrine will continue to be taught until the religious mood of our nation changes.

Those who are Christians reject the religion of secularism, therefore the Christian must turn from the public school to the Christian school. America has less Christian influence now than our founders ever conceived in their vision of separation between church and state. Al Janney, president of the American Association of Christian Schools, warns: "The Christian had better make up his mind that the gap between the Bible and the world is getting larger all the time. For many years the public school taught character education and reinforced the Protestant ethics that grew out of the Word of God. Now the public school is making a frontal attack on the Protestant ethics; therefore we had better answer their charges. And they make their attack by using our children; the young are the fodder for their mills, and the young come from us. They use our children to form a secular-humanistic America."

Secular Humanism Is Anti-Christian

During the past few years, Christians have considered the little red schoolhouse as the source of their child's education, while Christianity was taught at the family altar or in the church. However, the public school is no longer neutral, it is anti-Christian. When mandatory sex education was introduced without morality, the character and personality of children were threatened. A new post-Christian morality was enforced by sensitivity techniques that deny the sanctity of the person and is perpetuated by counselors who tell children, "Be cautious about telling your parents what you learn in school; they won't understand." Christians now face the philosophical question. Can education be divided into sacred and secular realm? Since the Bible teaches that all truth is God's truth, the dichotomy between sacred and secular education can no longer be tolerated.

Therefore, for a Christian to send his children to the public school is just as inconsistent as sending them to a

Unitarian Sunday School; they are learning the opposite of what is taught in the Word of God. The serious question needs to be raised, Can a Christian support the public schools of the United States? Al Janney maintains, "All week long our children are taught that what they learn in Sunday School is wrong, and when I complain about their frontal attack on Christianity, people ask, 'Why are you against the public schools?'"

The public schools that were begun by the Christians, have reversed fields, so that today children cannot read their Bibles, cannot pray, cannot have a Christmas service, cannot sing hymns, but they can read *Catcher in the Rye,* and *The Lord of the Flies,* and just about any other book that was condemned a few decades ago.

The question needs to be asked, Who has decided that pornography is good for our public schools and the Bible is bad? The battle between schools and church will center on the curriculum. Should a Christian permit his child to read that which is destructive?

Public Schools That Are Not

James Singleton, pastor of Tri-City Baptist Church, which founded the Tri-City Christian Academy, Tempe, Arizona, claims, "The Christian school has crept up on governmental agencies, which see the new schools as a new danger to their existence. Under the smokescreen of accusing Christian schools of shoddy work, they are trying to eliminate any opposition to the public schools through zoning requirements, the State Board of Health, and the fire marshal." Singleton believes that the real threat has to do with ultimate philosophy, i.e., the strong Christian is a disruptive element in a secular-humanistic society. The committed Christian is loyal to Jesus Christ. He desires to live by a life-style different from this world. "The committed Christian is willing to suffer mental-martyrdom, court battles, psychological pressure and disgrace. The committed Christian is a threat (or rebuke) by his superior character, to the product of the public school."

In this battle between the public school and the church, the question can be raised, Who controls the public schools? Are they, in fact, public? Al Janney looks at the growing bureaucracy of schools, noting they are controlled by state officials, not the public. "Up until now I have assumed that the government was a servant of the people, that government officials were paid by my taxes to serve me and my neighbors. This includes the public school teachers who are paid by tax money. However, it looks as though government has become the master of the people, rather than their servant." He refuses to call them "public" schools, calling them "federal" schools.

We can even raise the question concerning ultimate authority of the schools. To call them *public schools* assumes public control, wherein they reflect the desire of the community. However P.T.A. has less impact than ever before, and the school boards are losing their authority to teachers union. Al Janney voices parental objections: "We parents furnish the money, furnish the tools, furnish the pupils and then sit on our hand while the schools do what they please." He feels the public school officials expect us to "Vote our bond issue . . . raise taxes . . . and do what you're told." One would assume that the public schools of the United States are "of the people, by the people, and for the people." Janney questions if they are.

The Harvard Report, 1945, *General Education in a Free Society,* stated that the public school could not use theism or God as the unifying factor or ultimate force for a standard of morality in the child's life. If this opinion is accepted, should we educate the child in obedience to the state? Are we becoming a state-controlled society? It is possible to become a state-controlled nation, not by legislation but by education.

But educators reject the implication of state control, claiming the public schools reflect the general society. First, they claim to be objective, simply looking for the common denominator of our society. Un-adulterated objectivity is a myth and, like the emperor's new clothes, has no reality. Every educator teaches from his own perspective. Just as an historian can only be as accurate as the truthfulness of his sources, so an educator can only teach according to his sources. Since they have rejected Christianity, we cannot expect them to be neutral in examining its claims. The public schools are biased against Christianity and fight to rid themselves of its influence.

Public schools are built on compulsory education, and, with tongue in cheek, claim to be wholistic or pluralistic, including all aspects of society. However, they refuse to recognize the influence of Christianity or acknowledge its place in America. Therefore, the church cannot accept its academic excommunication; it must fight back by struggling for its existence. The Christian day school is its best weapon, and the battle is set.

Who Decided to Revolutionize Society?

The purpose of school is to communicate culture to the children, transmitting society from one generation to the next. However, modern educators have said that they are no longer interested in transmitting society, but revolutionizing it. The question needs to be asked, Who decided that the society needed to be revolutionized and who decides the new culture? If we are going to have a new world, should not the people, rather than the school, decide what it will be? Many public school educators feel they can better society against the will of the people and the will of the politicians. They can if we do not raise a serious question. Janney sees that, "We are in a battle for the future of our society, so we had better stop kidding ourselves about the potential good of the public school." He challenges, "We had better make up our minds to go back and do something about our stolen schools." Another journalist called it "The Great Training Robbery."

Conclusion

Recently an eighth-grade boy carried his Bible to school along with his other books. Not being ashamed of his faith, he put his black Bible on top of other books and displayed it proudly to his friends. The principal called him to the office and asked why he was carrying his Bible.

"As a testimony to my Lord," the young boy said.

"We don't want to start a riot." The principal reasoned with the boy that the Bible would bring out the agitators. "People will complain about Christianity in school," the principal said, noting that causing those problems would be the unchristian thing to do. However, during the same week, a teacher had assigned a lesson from *Playboy,* and they expected no problems from that.

NOTES

1. Steve Stewart, "For Learning or Segregation?" *The Atlanta Journal,* Atlanta, Ga., July 1, 1973, p. 20-A.

2. Sally Lofton, "Study Examines Private Schools," *Savannah Morning News,* Savannah, Ga., November 20, 1973, p. 10.

6 At the Peak
Of Their Decline

The world underwent extensive exploration and colonization during the Seventeenth Century, the time when the thirteen American colonies were founded. Judged from the world situation, the founding of the thirteen colonies was a minor incident in light of total expansion. Some might think that the establishment of Christianity in the thirteen colonies was merely an extension of western Europe, but the few hundred thousand people scattered along the eastern seaboard of North America had an ingredient to build a greater nation than any found on the Continent.

The vast majority of white settlers were Protestant, and they established a nation built on their faith. Only Maryland, among the thirteen colonies, was founded by English Roman Catholics. The Calvinistic Dutch settled in New Amsterdam; the Scotch and Irish Presbyterians settled in New Jersey; the English Quakers, a few English Baptists and Methodists settled in eastern Pennsylvania; the German-Lutherans, Moravians, Mennonites, Dunkards and the Reformed Church of Germany came to the valleys of Pennsylvania. Adherents to the Church of England settled in Virginia and the Southern colonies. Those with strong Presbyterian theology in their fiber settled the New England states. Separatists coming on the Mayflower in

1620 founded Plymouth. Puritans seeking religious liberty came in the next two decades, settling primarily in Connecticut. The Puritans and Separatists merged into a congregational pattern of church government.

Throughout New England a Christian commonwealth prevailed, where Christian principles controlled both church and state; all of society was permeated by Christian standards. The Bible was their supreme authority. The basis of law in the colony was to establish a civil code based upon the Bible. The church worship was the central core of colony life, and the sermon had a profound effect on political government throughout the colonial period. The religious devotion of families motivated them to carry out formal education to teach the young to read and perform simple skills in arithmetic. Once a week, the head of the household taught his children the shorter Catechism, testing his children to determine their understanding and memorization of answers. Fathers prayed with their children, guiding them in their spiritual living.

In 1635, the people of Boston voted in a town meeting to request a schoolmaster for their children. The following year, a college was set up, named after its first benefactor, John Harvard. Its founding purpose was "to advance learning, and perpetuate it to posterity; dreading to leave an illiterate ministry to the churches, when our present ministry shall lie in the dust." This first school of higher education was committed to academic excellence and set the standard for college education for the next 300 years. The printed entrance requirement for Harvard was:

When any scholar is able to understand Tully, or such like classical Latine author extempore, and make and speake true Latine in verse and prose, *suo ut aiunt marte;* and decline perfectly the paradigm's of nounes and verbes in the Greek tongue: Let him then and not before be capable of admission to the colledge.

To graduate from Harvard, a candidate not only had to read the Old and New Testament in their original languages, but to interpret them logically in the Latin tongue. In addition, he had to have a knowledge of logic, natural and moral philosophy, arithmetic, geometry and astronomy.

Preparing young men for college became a problem. The first law requiring each community to provide a school for its children, became one of the most significant laws in the history of Massachusetts: the well-known "Old Delueder, Satan Act" of 1647. This directed any town of fifty householders or more to establish a public school, which established the basis of public taxation for education. The law read,

One cheife project of ye old delueder, Satan, to keepe men from the knowledge of ye scriptures, as in former times by keeping them in an unknown tongue. [The express purpose of this act was] to instruct youth so farr as they shall be fited for ye university.

As a result, the religious motivation for establishing schools grew out of the church and as children were taught in the schools, the religious environment of the colonies grew. School was unquestionably religious in nature and purpose. The historian Cubberley notes, "Education for the young for membership in the church, and the perpetuation of a learned ministry for the congregation, from the first elicited the serious attention of these pioneer settlers." [1]

Often the same building was used for school and

church; many times the minister, by reason of his education, was both preacher and schoolmaster.

Elementary education designed for the poorer classes
was an apparently simple matter containing elements of
reading, writing the vernacular, arithmetic, and elements
of religious faith. The "Hornbooks" began with the prayer
of the Lord as the main text, inserted beneath the sheets
of transparent horn.

The *New England Primer* was introduced in 1690 and
for 125 years was the main reading book. The primer was
only 88 pages long, three and a quarter inches by four
and a half inches in size, but packed with a vast amount
of content: selections from the Bible, the Lord's Prayer,
the Apostles' Creed, illustrated alphabet, pictures of
animals with a rhyme under each, prayers for children,
grace before and after meals. Also included were prov-
erbs, poems, and pithy sayings. Some rural schools used
the primer well into this century. Some have claimed this
textbook had a greater influence for God and Christian
education than any ever written. Its best advertisement:
"It taught millions to read, and not one to sin." "In Adam's
fall we sinned all," began the alphabet of the primer.
Religion was at the core of the curriculum, as the following reading indicates.

That I was brought to know
The danger I was in,
By nature and by practice too
A wretched slave of sin,

That I was led to see
I can do nothing well
And whither shall a sinner flee
To save himself from hell?

In addition, the Catechism and the Bible were basic texts. Teachers were required to be capable of catechizing and leading pupils in the worship of God. Religious faith seemed more important than academic training of teachers. Every teacher was required to adhere closely to the religious life of the community and to attend church services regularly. Memorization was the primary pedagogical technique and pupils were to repeat their lessons when called upon by the teacher. The primary function of teachers was to assign lessons, discipline pupils, get them to study, and test their memories by calling upon them for recitation.

The Latin grammar school prepared young men for entrance into college. It also had a strong Christian emphasis. The rules of the grammar school at New Haven, Connecticut, were Christian at the core:

Then the scholars being called together the master shall every morning begin his work with a short prayer for a blessing in his labors and their learning . . .

The scholars behave themselves at all times, especially in school time, with due reverence to their master, and with sobriety and quietness among themselves, without fighting, quarreling, or calling one another or any other, bad names, or using bad words in cursing, taking the name of God in vain, or other profane, obscene, or corrupt speeches, which if any do, that the master forthwith give them due correction . . .

That if any of the school boys be observed to play, sleep, or behave themselves rudely, or irreverently, or be in any way disorderly at meeting on the Sabbath Day, or at any time of the public worships of God, that upon information or complaint thereof to the due concretion of the offender or offenders, the master shall give them due corrections to the degree of the offense . . .

That all the Latin scholars and all other of the boys of competent age and capacity give the master an account of one passage or sentence at least of the sermons of the foregoing Sabbath on the second day morning. And that from 1 to 3 in the afternoon of every last day of the week be improved by the masters in catechizing of his scholars that are capable.[2]

Out of the Latin grammar school evolved the American academy in the middle of the Eighteenth Century, finally growing into the public high school at the end of the Nineteenth Century.

Since the local government controlled public schools, the varying amount of influence that church bodies had on town council and political authorities resulted in varying amounts of religious influence in the public schools. With the growth of the American frontier, the emergence of a middle class, the desire to separate church and state, and the need for leaders in a growing united political republic, public school education began to take on a broader scope during the later colonial period.

In 1749, the "general law of the colony of Massachusetts Bay" passed an apparently broader concept of public education.

(1) to teach the children and youth to read perfectly the English tongue, (2) to teach them a knowledge of laws respecting capital crimes, (3) to catechize children and servants in the grounds and principles of religion at least once a week and (4) to bring up children and apprentices in some "honest, lawful selling, labor or employment," for themselves and the commonwealth.[3]

These laws included other objectives for education than had been previously articulated, i.e. preparation of young people for membership in the church and the preparation of a learned ministry. Within a hundred years after public schools were founded upon Christian principles, they were moving toward secularized content and purpose. At the same time new textbooks appeared, replacing religious material with more secular matters. One of these books was Dilworth's *A New Guide to the English Tongue,* which was a forerunner of Webster's blue-back spelling book published in 1783. After the first appearance of secular or semisecular textbooks, the religious and moral content of all readers gradually decreased.[4]

After the Revolutionary War, the nation began taking on a new personality, and the schools followed suit. The schools were still local institutions, designed to meet the specific needs of a small segment of the community. They still served largely to instill religious orthodoxy in children. Much of the curriculum was removed from everyday life. Also, the schools reflected and perpetuated a dual class system, with the vernacular elementary school tending to confine itself to the lower class, while the Latin secondary schools served the upper classes.

However, there were monumental changes in the nation, bringing a transition in the schools. The coming of Catholic immigrants; increased association with the tolerance of individuals of religious sects toward one another; scientific discoveries; widening intellectual horizons due to books, periodicals, and newspapers; increase in material prosperity; a growing separation of church and state; failure of the old church-town governments to function; and the development of new economic and civic interests. Education moved away from exclusive religious preparation and began concerning itself with secular matters. The aim of education was changing.

A new set of principles of the establishment of government evolved for public schools including political and educational aims along with religious aims. The nation came to believe that human life could be greatly improved and that the government could be used to bring about such improvements by the exaltation of the rights of the individual. Rather than establishing a religious nation, the Declaration of Independence adopted the principal of life, liberty, and the pursuit of happiness as inalienable rights of every person simply because he was a human being. However, God was not ruled out of the affairs of men. The founding fathers believed the nation could not be founded apart from faith in Him. Finally, most important to the development of this chapter, the new nation believed that education was the indispensable means of prompting and perpetuating the general welfare. Hence, education took on a messianic quality in the United States. Even today there is a subconscious attitude that any problem in society can be solved through education if schools are given enough money and time to work out a solution.

After the Revolutionary War, debates increased over who should pay for schools, who should control schools, and what should be taught in the schools. The country was gradually accepting the principle of public-controlled education, maintained by public funds. This was a long, hard-fought battle, and there were varying rates of progress toward the goal of public taxation. Generally, New England, with its colonial tradition of public-supported schools, moved rapidly toward compulsory support. The Middle and Southern states displayed less interest in education during the colonial period and consequently moved slowly toward public support, often times begrudgingly.[5]

Horace Mann, an outstanding figure in this period of

education, was secretary of the Massachusetts Board of Education from 1831-1848. He strengthened the control of education by the states. He was more instrumental than any other one person in taking the control of schools out of the hands of local authorities, moving it to the state level. Since local churches had less influence in the state capitol than in the small town council, religion played a smaller influence in public schools. Also, acceptance of the principle of public tax-supported schools minimized the influence of local sectarian groups in the control over education aims and content.[6]

During the early nineteenth century many American people were driven to the conclusion that if teaching of religion could not be carried on in the public schools without sectarian strife, it would have to be eliminated. As a result, church leaders began to view the school as inhospitable to religious interpretation of morals. They began to look elsewhere for a vehicle to teach their faith.[7]

Impart the reluctance with which the decision was reached, was tempered by the hope that the rising Sunday School movement would supply sufficient cover to what was lacking in the public schools.[8]

However, the public schools were not completely irreligious; the Puritan/Protestant ethic still held a primary place in the public school curriculum. But other aims were being added, such as: strengthening the mind's power to reason logically, universal literacy, education for citizenship, vocational and practical competence, and individual success. As the aim of education broadened, the common school curriculum was broadened. The threefold development was: subjects providing the knowledge and skills necessary for the responsible exercise of citizenship, subjects providing suitable religious and moral training, and subjects providing loyalty to the republic.[9]

Horace Mann displayed an overwhelming concern for the implications of teaching religious morals in the public school. He tried to establish among sectarian denominations a common faith to be taught in the schools, but found none. As a result, he brought his scornful rebuke on religion in the public schools, stating:

It is easy to see that the experiment would not stop with having half a dozen conflicting creeds taught by authority of law in the differing schools of the same town or vicinity. Majorities will change in the same place. One sect may have the ascendancy today; another, tomorrow . . . this year the everlasting fires of hell will burn to terrify the unrepentent; next year, and without any repentence, its eternal flame will be extinguished, to be rekindled forever or to be quenched forever as it may be decided at the annual town meeting.[10]

Even though Horace Mann championed the cause of driving religion from the public schools, he favored ethical instruction in its place.

Mann forwarded moral and ethical instruction in the schools to the fullest extent possible without invading those rights of conscience which are established by the laws of God and guaranteed by the state . . . about this he said, "Against a tendency to leave extremes, the beautiful and sublime truth of ethics and natural religion have a poising power.[11]

The decline of the content of morality in the curriculum of schools is clearly seen in Parkin's investigation of the moral and religious content of 1,291 American school readers, covering the period from 1776 to 1920.[12]

    1716-1786   100 percent moral and religious emphasis
    1786-1825   50 percent moral and religious emphasis

1825-1880   21 percent moral and religious emphasis
1916-1920   5 percent moral and religious emphasis

During this period, women evolved into the position of teacher in the American scene. Perhaps this grew out of district control of public schools. All too often, officials were concerned with one thing in the management of schools—economy. Women were paid less salary than men. Also, the Jacksonian concept of public office prevailed: that is, anyone could hold any office with little or no training as qualifications.

Quite often the teacher was simply the daughter or some other unmarried female relative of the district prudential man. She had completed the common school, and in a very limited number of incidences she had attended a local academy for a short period of time.[13]

As a result, the teacher resorted to hearing lessons and providing little help beyond that found in the textbook. There was little difference between *school-keeping* and *school-teaching*. Teachers worked in an environment where all instruction was minimized by default rather than through conscious efforts to ignore the spiritual. In this growing spiritual vacuum, the older order of religious morals tended to be replaced by a growing secular religion.

Many Causes

The diminished Christian emphasis in public schools was the result of many natural and humanistic causes. But back of the decline of Christianity in the public schools is the antithesis that has been characteristic from the beginning—the human opposition to divine truth. Every system, no matter how imperfect, begins to decline the moment it is founded, just as a baby begins to die the moment he is born. On the other side of the coin, truth is always eroded by error and does not remain in its pure form.

The years following the Civil War (1865) witnessed a phenomenal expansion of the American educational system. In effect, schools grew from an uncertain infancy in 1865 to maturity by 1945. During this time a vast majority of American children attended elementary school, some for shorter, others for longer periods of their youth. Institutions to train teachers came into existence. New institutions such as the junior high schools, junior colleges and land-grant colleges were established to meet the specific needs of groups of individuals. Compulsory school attendance brought many of the young of this country into the schools, and with the influx of all kinds of pupils with various needs, various aims, and various backgrounds came a new concept of education. Preparation for trade and vocational training became an increasing part of the high school programs. Active training for self-expression and citizenship entered the halls of education which had formerly been devoted largely to transmitting knowledge and moral precepts.

State Control

Each state still controlled the process of public education. The growth in compulsory attendance laws during this time in part laid the foundation for the greatness of the United States. But with the required attendance came a host of new problems. Thousands of recalcitrant or slow learners were forced to attend school. In former times, they would have been dropped because they could not complete the curriculum. Now they became the responsibility of the school for a minimum of attendance. Also, the school was forced to enroll many new groups of children for whom the traditional program had no particular meaning, such as blacks, immigrants, and other ethnic groups who were brought into public school classes. In effect, compulsory attendance forced differentiation of school purposes and curricula in order that the different educational needs of the heterogeneous school population might be taught.

Compulsory Attendance

Compulsory attendance also had a deep effect on the content of moral instruction in the school. No longer could the small sectarian group force its doctrine on the school system. Moral education had been expressed in terms of the majority of the American public, now the majority was no longer Protestant-sectarian. Those who advocated teaching religion in the public schools did not surrender without a fight. After the Civil War, many court decisions were handed down which affected moral instruction in the public school. Butts and Cremin summarized some of these decisions:

Some courts ruled that the Bible was not sectarian in instruction, provided it was read without comment and students who objected were excused from taking part. Such decisions obviously reflected the feeling that non-sectarian religious teaching was essential in a school program.

Other courts, however, held that reading the King James Bible —a sectarian version in the eyes of Catholics and Jews and non-believers—violated freedom of conscience, was thereby unconstitutional, and should therefore be prohibited.[14]

As a result, the extent of moral education in the public schools decreased at the last part of the nineteenth cen-

tury. Some educators call this a period of vacuum because religious and moral education were neglected. But
getting religion out of the schools brought other problems,
especially since many less educable children, forced by
compulsory attendance laws to attend school, created
havoc in the learning environment. These children needed
to be taught commonly accepted values to prepare for
citizenship. Educators were forced to concern themselves
with character education. If the public schools were
destructive, what would society be like? United States
Commissioner of Education Harris stated in 1892:

Religious education has almost ceased in the public schools
and is rapidly disappearing from the program of college and
preparatory schools. At present, on examination of the legal
provision of the reading of the Bible in the public schools,
we find that in only a few states is permitted the formal reading
of the Bible and the recitation of the Lord's Prayer. The general situation seems to be that the law permits the reading of
the Bible in most schools if no one objects, but forbids it if an
objection is raised.[15]

Spiritual Need

Many American educators recognized the spiritual need
of children, but they also realized the American school
is not the place to teach religious morals. They began to
examine the question, "What can be done by the public
schools to teach morals?" The suggestions of Horace Mann
that morals be centered around citizenship and a basic
nonsectarian group of commonly accepted values began
to find its way into the thinking of educators.[16] Mann had
given birth to a concept of American morality seventy-
five years before the public was willing to receive it. A
sectarian concept of morality slowly evolved. Based on

the Protestant/Puritan ethic, a new morality of God without sectarian doctrine was accepted by the public school.

In 1892, Charles De Garmo advocated the need of moral instructions:

The most universal interest in ethical training leads to the conclusion that our former standpoint of near intellectuality in school education is being shifted to one that takes more cognizance of developing moral character.[17]

De Garmo went on to recommend three areas of study: (1) a humanistic core of studies having a distinct ethical content in literature and history; (2) a group of major studies have no specific ethical content; and (3) an economic core of studies emphasizing man's relationship with the past in order to build for the future with the universal study of geography to bind these three together.[18]

Teaching Religionless Morality Through Direct Methods

The religionless morality viewed citizenship education as intimately tied to moral education. However, the question was raised, How could citizenship/morality be instructed in the public schools? Some held that religionless-morals could be taught through an authoritarian approach with conventional classroom techniques. George Palmer advocated:

In systematic teaching of ethics in the classroom lies the best means of enlarging the moral influence of the school. This belief expressed itself in the provision of regular courses in "morals and manners" and again "ethics and behavior" and again "civics and the like." [19]

Palmer went on to describe a profile of the school where religionless-morality was practiced. It was an ideal environment for education.

That schools where neatness, courtesy simplicity obtained, where enthusiasm goes with mental exactness, thoroughness of work with interest and absence of artificiality with refinement; where sneaks, liars, loafers, pretenders, rough persons are despised; where teachers who refuse to be mechanical held sway—that school is engaged in moral training all day long.[20]

In 1909, the Character Development League of New York City initiated a plan of character education using as its basis the biographies of great men. A book written especially for this purpose include biographies and pictures.[21] Different traits were suggested for each grade in training examples.

In 1914, the Pathfinders of America, an organization founded by J. F. Wright, and unique in that it had no official connection with the public school, mirrored the belief that character education should be recognized as a special subject with special teachers in just the same way as any other school subject. In general the plan consisted of a basic talk by a trained teacher on such a topic as "Be faithful to yourself," "The guide of life," "How to be happy," followed by a meeting of pupils, where they could discuss and make application of the points mentioned in the address.

Codes of morality were common during the early part of this century. Perhaps the best known of these was the Hutchins code which appeared in 1916. The code's excellence, plus the publicity it received as winner of the $5,000 prize offered by an anonymous donor through the Character Education Institution, commended it to many people. This code is composed of eleven "laws," including the law of self-control, of good health, of kindness, of duty, and of loyalty. Daily discussion periods of ten to fifteen minutes were recommended for public schools to communicate these values.

In 1924, Superintendent Burke of the Boston Schools, assisted by ministers and teachers, developed a "Course in Citizenship through Character Development." [22] In this plan, fifteen minutes a day were used to present and discuss each character trait, with two weeks devoted to a trait. The apparent purpose of this course was to instill an objective standard in students.

During the 1920's pupil manuals were developed in many large school systems for use in moral instruction. The Pittsburgh Plan developed morals by emphasizing each year one major trait, such as loyalty and ambition, via stories, illustrations, and questions. The twelve booklets were called "Guideposts to Character." [23]

Character Education, a manual for the teachers of Oregon, emphasized the progressive nature of virtue. Seventy-five traits were classified into three columns representing three successive stages of development—the first for the primary child, the second for the intermediate child, and the third for the upper grades. For instance, obedience in the first column, conformity in the second column, and cooperation in the last. In the last column would be the ultimate character objective.[24]

A survey by Alvin H. Fishback in 1928 on the status of courses for moral education in the United States revealed that seventeen states and the District of Columbia required character education. Twelve states did not have state requirements, but reported that character instruction was carried on in cities and school districts.[25]

The workbook idea on moral training of children came into use in the 1930's, placing a manual in the hand of each student to help instruct him in character education. An example is *Conduct Problems for the Junior High School Grades,* Set A (1930) and Set B (1931).[26] Each set contained fifty problems for discussion, wherein a short incident was related, significant questions asked, and answers written in the manual by the students. These answers were discussed in homeroom, and the pupil's final reaction was recorded. Apparently the workbook idea marked the begining of the end of direct methods of teaching morals to the public school pupil. Although some teachers may have still applied the direct method, this approach was on its way to extinction by the Second World War.

Teaching Religionless-Morality Through Indirect Methods

Although direct methods of instructing morals were introduced at the turn of the century, reaction against any type of authoritarian instruction became stronger. Some educators maintained indirect instruction was more effective. In 1896, Wilson L. Gill organized "The School Republic" in a school on the lower side of New York. Each room was organized as a complete city, with the officers and committees usually found in municipal government; each had its particular responsibility in connection with certain activities of the "city" and the pupil citizens within it. Democracy permeated the entire school, indirectly preparing children for the moral framework into which he would be graduated.[27]

Teaching values indirectly through the student council was a growing trend. It was argued that morals could be "caught" better than "taught." As a result, children were reared in a democratic environment, with a view of communicating to them the value of "life, liberty and the pursuit of happiness."

By 1925, a survey showed that 39.3 percent of the high

schools had "pupil government," and a similar survey two years later found the percentage had increased to 45 percent. Earle Rugg, after an investigation of 191 schools selected at random, estimated that 90 percent of them were making an effort to teach morals indirectly through the student council.[28]

During this period the idea of the home room in the junior and senior high school came into existence as an avenue for teaching morals. The teacher in the home room was assigned the same aim as the guidance program, to help students in their self-development and self-direction, hence teaching them character education.[29] Consequently, a new philosophy in moral training no longer concerned itself with just keeping a standard; morality was a way of life or training for citizenship. John Dewey spoke out against the traditional school and its authoritarian moral instruction:

We need to see that moral principles are not arbitrary, that they are not "transcendental", that the term "moral" does not designate a special region or portion of life. We need to translate the moral into the conditions and forces of our community life, and into the impulses and habits of individuals.[30]

The groundwork was laid for a good society, without God. Educators wanted a liberated mind without eternal laws. The philosophic ideas of religionless morality continued until the 60's, then the public schools ran into trouble.

CONCLUSION

During the colonial period of our nation, strong emphasis was placed on religious education of the young. The church was the prevailing founder and sponsor of education. Since God was recognized as the source of truth, He was the center of the educational process. Character was built in the students, although never the educational aim. Truth was taught as an absolute standard.

Al Janney, president of the American Association of Christian Schools, commented in a recent speech on this period of education:

Between 1600 and 1776 our nation existed without boards of education, federally subsidized schools, teacher training colleges, and federal judges to tell us how to educate children. During that time our nation produced a generation of people who wrote the Constitution, the best document ever framed for a nation: they desired freedom, decided they would not be taxed without representation, fought against the greatest empires in the world, and forged out a nation. They built one of the greatest societies ever known to man, that produced the greatest good to the greatest number of people at the least cost—simply because families and churches decided that their children would have a godly education.

Between the Revolutionary and Civil Wars, the scope of scholars expanded. Parents valued education for their children, and America moved toward the concept of universal training for every child. The purpose of schools evolved with changing times; pupils were no longer prepared only for church goals; they were educated to take a place in a young, growing nation. The schools were religious but not sectarian, they were authoritarian but not controlled by church doctrine. But the trend was clear; with each succeeding generation the schools were drifting.

After the Civil War, compulsory education forced greater secularism upon the schools; yet educators saw the need for character training. America still wanted the

Protestant/Puritan ethic inherent in colonial schools, yet they didn't want its strict adherence nor did they want biblical Christianity, which was its basis. After the turn of the century, educators placed much emphasis on character education, but eventually those who opposed authoritarian methods and an objective standard grew in influence. Character education continued until the 1960's, but its erosion was inevitable. Without a foundation the traditional ethic gave way to the post-American morality of the 1970's. Since morality is the cohesive that keps a society together, it is questionable if the new morality can hold America together.

First, the church lost its place in the schools. Next, God was dispensed from the classroom; and during the last decade the public schools have lost their character.

Therefore we ask, "Have the public schools 'had it'?"

NOTES

1. Ellwood P. Cubberley, *The History of Education* (New York: Houghton Mifflin Co., 1926), p. 357.

2. Adapted from Barnard's American Journal of Education, IV, 710 as found in C. B. Eavey, *History of Christian Education* (Chicago: Moody Press, 1964), p. 197.

3. Quoted by Charles H. Dent, "Opportunities for Character Education in Elementary Schools" (Unpublished Master's Thesis, Southern Methodist University, Dallas, 1940), p. 11.

4. Harry McKown, *Character Education* (New York: McGraw-Hill Book Co., 1935), p. 74.

5. Freeman Butts, Lawrence A. Cremin, *A History of Education in The American Culture* (New York: Henry Holt and Company, 1953), p. 244ff.

6. *Ibid.*, p. 275.

7. Truda LaGrone, "The Present Status of the teaching of Morals in the Public Schools of Texas" (Unpublished Master's Thesis, Southern Methodist University, Dallas, 1927), p. 13.

8. American Council on Education, "The Relation of Religion to Public Education, A Study prepared by the Committee on Religious Education" (Washington, D. C.: American Council on Education, April, 1947), Vol. XI, Number 26, p. 7.

9. Butts and Cremin, pp. 267-269. See this section for a discussion of the aims of education during 1779 to 1865.

10. Raymond B. Culver, *Horace Mann and Religion in the Massachusetts Public Schools* (New Haven: Yale University Press, 1929), p. 208.

11. American Council on Education, p. 8.

12. McKown, p. 74.

13. Butts and Cremin, p. 286.

14. *Ibid.*, p. 436.

15. W. P. Harris, Report of 1892 to the National Education Association, p. 10.

16. American Council on Education, p. 8.

17. Charles De Garmo, "Moral, A Working Basis for the Correlation of Studies," *Educational Review*, XV (May, 1893), p. 459.

18. Charles De Garmo, "Moral Training through the Common Branches," Proceedings of the National Education Association, XXXIII, 165-173.

19. George H. Palmer, *Ethical and Moral Instruction in Schools,* (New York: Houghton Mifflin Co., 1909), p. 8.

20. *Ibid.*, p. 41.

21. J. T. White, "Character Lessons in American Biography," (New York: The Character Development League, 1909).

22. School Document 10, 1925. Boston Public Schools, Boston, Massachusetts.

23. *Guideposts to Character,* Pittsburgh Public Schools, American Book Company, 1924.

24. *Character Education,* Superintendent of Public Instruction, Salem, Oregon.

25. Elvin H. Fishback, "Character Education in the United States," *Elementary School Journal,* XXXIX (1928), 277-279.

26. E. H. Fishback, and E. A. Kirkpatrick, *Conduct Problems for the Junior High School Grades,* D. C. Heath and Company, 1930.

27. McKown, p. 85.

28. *Twenty-fifth Yearbook,* National Society for the Study of Education, Chapter XI, 1926.

29. Elmer L. Towns, "An Analysis of the Implications of Teaching Morals in the Public Schools" (Unpublished Master's Thesis, Southern Methodist University, Dallas, 1958), pp. 35-36, 55-64.

30. John Dewey, *Moral Principles in Education* (New York: Houghton Mifflin Co., 1909), p. 58.

7 Are We Approaching A Post-American Ethic?

Men constructing a building first erect a scaffolding as a frame for work on the structure. The scaffolding is temporary and is removed when the building is completed. The founding fathers attempted to establish a Christian nation and church-controlled schools. These met a desperate need and served the purpose of erecting a nation built on Christian principles and influenced by biblical patterns. Yet the nation should not have become a Christian commonwealth nor should the schools have remained church-dominated. Otherwise, our nation would not have been founded on religious liberty. The founding fathers were rearing the necessary scaffolding from which the building (the United States) would be constructed. The building is much more important than the scaffolding.

During the church-dominated days of schools, sectarian indoctrination was their main purpose (see chapter six). Shortly after the establishment of the schools, church-indoctrination was replaced with community-related instruction.[1] However, not all church influence was pushed out of the schools; the Protestant/Puritan ethic remained for over 200 years. Upon this ethic the Bill of Rights was conceived, and it was the driving motive behind the Declaration of Independence and the Constitution.

Church indoctrination was the scaffolding, the Protestant/Puritan ethic was the building it constructed. The *building* was the American way of life, it should endure.

But those who have worked effectively to extricate religion from the public schools have not only taken down the scaffolding, they are destroying the building in the process. Public school educators openly attack any vestigial remains of Christianity, such as cleanliness, self-respect, unity, discipline, orderliness, or academic excellence. Little do they realize the American ethic is under attack. This chapter examines the Protestant/Puritan ethic, noting that its erosion from education will have a corresponding influence on the nation.

Theologians agree that Christian principles have less effect now than in the past. Some have noted the United States has evolved to the post-Christian era. Americans live beyond the consciousness of God. Humanistic-secular values have replaced the Protestant/Puritan ethic. This chapter maintains the American ethic is synonymous with the Protestant/Puritan ethic. It is the spiritual unity and composite dream of the good life. As we witness a post-Christian age, we also witness the rise of the post-American ethic. The post-American ethic is destroying the historical purpose of our nation and its dream of the good life.

The public schools have been the main "carrier" of the American way of life. Robert Havinghurst, one of America's leading educator-sociologists, notes, "It can be said most accurately that the societal value changes are *causing* changes in education." [2]

What Do Schools Communicate?

We cannot talk about public schools without dealing with society. Children come from many different social groupings. Teachers have various backgrounds and environments. Each community has its own personality. Its subculture is different from other communities. As a result, each school is a society different in its personality, reflecting different attitudes toward its children. It is this diversity which the public schools must transmit and reflect. Yet, if the similarities of society become too great, it will be impossible to (1) reflect society in the public schools, and (2) transmit a diverse society on to future generations.

When people share common ways of behaving and believing, they are a *social group*. Their commonality makes them a group rather than just an incidental collection of people. People become a *culture* when a large number share similar behavior and beliefs.

By "culture," we mean people with similar patterns of thought, and similar behavior; their etiquette, language, institutions, values, attitudes, and systems of knowledge fall within the same pattern. A culture is a patterned way of life in a society.

Culture never just happens. Man creates culture. It is a human production. It is an inherent drive of culture to transmit what man has learned and what man has created to his children, that they might carry on that culture. The complex society shared by all Americans is a human production. We are the sum-total of all that our forefathers have made us. Just as it was their duty to pass society on to us, so it is our duty to pass it on to our children.

Within every culture, there are groups of people that have a *subculture* all their own. In America, we share a common language, use the same monetary system, dress somewhat alike, and have certain understandings by which we live in harmony. But when groups of individuals express their uniqueness (historical background, religious life, ethnic culture), they are a subculture. The strength of our nation has been to incorporate varying subcultures without losing the dominant identity of our society.

America has been known as a nation of similarity. When foreigners immigated to our shores, they wanted to act and think like Americans. They wanted to assume the social patterns of the new nation. Yet those from other cultures could not completely cut off their past. They kept the warmth and dignity of their former subculture while assimilating a new American life style. As a result, Americans live in essentially the same kinds of houses, eat similar food, dress the same, furnish their houses similarly, enjoy the same kind of literature, seek similar recreation, and laugh at the same jokes.

America is a social culture, and individuals can learn this culture just by living in the United States. The historical purpose of the public school is to speed and enrich the process, communicating this cultural heritage from one generation to another. Therefore, we can call the school a socializing agency, operating within the orbit of the wider community. If the public schools reflected the American culture, there would be no problem. However, the school is creating itself into a culture, entirely different from the society in which it exists. Most educators recognize:

The school has a subculture of its own—a complex set of beliefs, values and traditions, ways of thinking and behaving—that differentiate it from other social institutions. The function of the school is education; and all the personnel of the school, from the kindergartener to the high school senior, from the office clerk to the superintendent, are present to further that function.[3]

But we can question if the public schools are committed to that traditional purpose of education, at least academic education. Public schools have developed their own religionless society, secular humanism, which is a religion (see chapter 5).

Folklore and myth, tradition, taboo, magic rites, ceremonials of all sorts, collective representations, participation mystiques, all abound in the front yard of every school, and occasionally they creep upstairs and are incorporated into the moral formal positions of school life.

There are in the school, complex rituals of personal relationships, a set of folks way, morays and irrational sanctions, or moral code based upon them. There are games which are sublimated wars, teams, and elaborate sets of ceremonies concerning them. There are traditions, and traditionalists waging their world-old battle against innovators . . . all these things make up a world that is different from a world of adults.[4]

In the public schools, children learn the process of their society, how to live in the world after graduation. The socialization process changes infants into adults, gradually making them into Americans. By the process of *socialization,* a child assumes a total way of life. In the past, the child learned how to read, to respect authority, the position of women in society, and the place of grandparents. Girls learned to be "graceful" and young men learned the limits of strength. Attitudes toward cleanliness, reverence of institutions, and fidelity are assimilated at the subconscious level. Socialization is defined:

Socialization has also active and constructive aspects; it produces growth; it encourages, nurtures, stimulates, and motivates; it produces an infinite variety of desires and strivings in the individual; it leads to development and achievement of all kinds. It cultivates certain potentialities in the individual, and at the same time, suppresses others. In this sense, socialization has both a creative as well as inhibiting effect upon the individual.

In overall terms, then, socialization is both a molding and creating process, in which the culture of the group is brought to bear upon the infant, and in which the individual's thought, feeling, and behavior gradually but continually change and develop in accordance with the values set by society.[5]

The key word above is *values*. The process of socialization cannot operate without values. Men live in harmony when they prize the same items in society. If men do not prize or place different values upon various functions, then society collapses. Society must place the same importance on money, language, the future, privacy and integrity. A society is essentially a set of warranted predictions made by its members about one another's behavior. In the social concept of group living, individuals must make verbal or non-verbal commitments to one another based on a mutual trust (prediction) that others will continue to act in a predictable role or pattern. Society begins to crumble when individuals are not able to predict one another's social reaction. Without the predictable behavior patterns, men are not able to trust one another to accomplish personal goals or group goals.

The Protestant/Puritan value system that has been communicated by our schools for the last 300 years has been driven out of our public schools in the past few years. The following questions have not been raised, much less answered. Who determined that the traditional values of our nation should be changed? Since these values have made us into a great nation, should they be changed? Is there a new value to take their place or are schools functioning in a valueless society? (The question is rhetorical. There is no such thing as a valueless society.) Can a new system of values hold society together or motivate our nation to continue its present momentum?

The United States has been a Christian nation in name only, although it has been greatly influenced by Christian principles. It would be inconsistent with the facts to call America Christian. Our nation has committed too many un-Christian acts, it has too many non-Christian citizens, and it does not express unique Christian aims in its Declaration of Independence or its Constitution. But the men who formed this nation were deeply influenced by a Christian environment. Although we are not a Christian nation, we have been greatly influential by our Christian heritage and Christian churches have made an impact on our people.

Some of our original settlers tried to make the colonies a Christian commonwealth (i.e., Cotton Mather), but sensible heads prevailed. The First Amendment assured religious liberty, that we would have a nation both free from the control of religion and free to exercise any religion. But from our settlers came values and understandings, the necessary agreements that makes society operate. These understandings are usually not vocalized, yet people in society govern their social interactions by them. Social values that held society together was the American value because it was expressive of their culture and grew out of a Christian heritage. The Protestant/Puritan ethic is synonymous with the American ethic, the social understanding on which the United States society is built.

There has been much discussion about the Protestant/Puritan ethic but little actual research has been done into its nature and contribution. The liberal press attacks it, the public school tries to extricate it, and Christians take it for granted. Only when it is taken away does the Christian feel its loss, then he wants it, but still can't articulate what it is he values.

In research for this volume, no workable definition of a Protestant or Puritan ethic could be found, although it is the foundation on which this nation was built. Actually there is a difference between the Protestant and Puritan ethics, although they are similar because both arise from Biblical Christianity. They will be defined separately for careful study, but will be used synonymously throughout this volume. The following definitions were created to give meaning to this chapter.

The Protestant ethic maintains the individual is responsible for ordering his actions in keeping with continuing truth, which is reflective of God; that institutions such as family, government, and the church are given by God for the good of its members; and that the objective of man is to employ his intellect, talents and strength to improve himself, family, nation and church; and that failure to complete one's obligations has its own built-in judgment in addition to extrinsic punishment.

Out of the Protestant ethic grew the following concepts. (1) *A success-oriented society* built on achievement, therefore, high schools sponsor football to encourage competitiveness. (2) *A work-ethic* where individuals sought gainful employment for both livelihood and self expression, therefore schools have prized education claiming it will lead to better jobs. (3) *Patriotism* where the individual both respects and is loyal to his nation, as a result, schools have the pupils salute the flag. (4) *Integrity* where the individual's word was his pledge, upon which others could depend. Schools have communicated this ethic, and students who cheat on tests are punished. (5) *Law and order* because society is built on God who ordered the world and without laws the individual would not have the opportunity to achieve his station in life nor make his contribution to society. Therefore, students who run in the halls, ditch class, or break other rules have been punished. These basic rules flow from the ethic which holds society together.

The Puritan ethic maintains the individual's personality reflects a holy sinless God and man's chief responsibility in life is to govern himself according to the standards of purity found in Scripture, and that purity should extend to every facet of personal life, thoughts, attitudes, actions and physical demeanor, and that cleanliness should extend to the family, community and business life. Since sexual purity is the ultimate value, any deviation is a grave offence in society.

Out of the Puritan ethic has grown the following habits: (1) *Personal cleanliness,* therefore expensive shower rooms are constructed for cleaning up after gymnastics (2) *Pure communication,* cleanliness was prized and students who have used words symbolizing filth have been punished in the past. (3) *Pure relationships* were assumed, those who stole, cheated, raped, or did violence were judged according to the severity of their crime. (4) *Clean personal demeanor,* therefore dirty clothes were censured by teachers. Clean teeth, hands and faces were held up as an example. (5) *Sex is private and personal,* therefore students were censured for language, jokes, actions that deviated from sexual cleanliness. Courses in sex education can be considered a transgression against personal privacy.

One of the best expressions of the Protestant/Puritan ethic was the Boy Scout oath, each Scout raising his right hand and repeating;

On my honor I will do my best to do my duty to God and my country and to obey the Scout Law; to help other people at all times; to keep myself physically strong, mentally awake, and morally straight.

A careful examination will show that the Scout oath was not sectarian oriented; the Fundamental Baptist, devout Catholic, or Orthodox Jew could adopt the Scout pledge and not violate his conscience. It was an American ethic, not a Christian ethic. The 12 laws in Scouting applied the same ethic. Once again, any religion could adopt its use. A Scout is trustworthy, loyal, helpful, friendly, courteous, kind, obedient, cheerful, thrifty, brave, clean, and reverent. As a result, the Scout pledged himself to be loyal to country and reverent to God. The American ethic was aware of the existence of God.

The following outline has been used by the author in sociology courses to explain the Protestant/Puritan ethic. The best symbolism is WASP (White Anglo Saxon Protestant), the whipping boy of the liberal press. In their magnification of minorities, the WASP has been vilified. In a democracy, the vocal minorities have rights the same as the silent majority. The WASP has been the seat of suggestibility for American values. As the WASP becomes a minority, his voice will become more vocal, hence many will find the WASP still has a sting. The following characterizations are not suggested as the ultimate explanation of the American ethic, but are given to help the reader understand the foundation of the public schools.

A Description of the Protestant/Puritan Ethic

1. *Belief in God and attendance of church.*—Since the nation was founded out of religious motivation, Americans have lived under an awareness of God. Our coins

are stamped "In God We Trust." The pledge to the flag asks for allegiance of citizens to "one nation under God." On the Tomb of the Unknown Soldier is inscribed "Known Only to God." Our presidents are sworn into office by use of a Bible.

2. *Belief in personal cleanliness.*—America has spent more money on mouth wash, laundry soap, and paper towels than any other nation, simply because it prizes purity. In the past, purity of body, thoughts, language, and actions has been prized. That standard is changing. The advocates of the post-Christian morality claim that obscenities are acceptable. What were formerly called deviations are now pure. The wave of student rebellion seems to zero in on cleanliness. The draggy jeans, dirty hair, tie-dye clothes may appear harmless on the surface, but seem to be a trend. Schools were once kept orderly and clean. Pupils were reprimanded for dropping trash on the floor or littering the school yard. Today, some high school hallways are streamed with waste once untolerated in school, still unacceptable in most of our homes.

3. *Belief in thrift.*—Our nation has placed value upon wise use of money. Since time is money, neither should be thrown away. Also credit is money and should be valued. A correct use of money will ultimately lead to economic success. Just as money begets money and its offsprings beget more and more, so the more money the person has, the more it produces, bringing about wealth. Max Weber says Ben Franklin was the personification of the Protestant ethic because Franklin taught the value of saving money and that a young man should keep an exact account of both time and expenses, because there is no future without saving for it.[6]

4. *Intellect should control one's life.*—Americans have

grown accustomed to handling their differences through understanding rather than physical might. Society is based on a rational relationship. Children have been taught that emotions (anger, passion, greed) should not control their life. Traditionally, intellect reflected mastery of eternal truth. The intellectual person was prized, and the Ph.D. was elusive. Therefore, the intellectual approach to problems was the proper way to govern one's life.

5. *Aggression is expressed in socially accepted ways.*—When children fought on the playground, they were corrected. Physical aggression was not valued unless it was disciplined by socially accepted ways, such as boxing, football, and other contact sports. However, there was a time when boxing was socially unacceptable because of its physical abuse. Children were conditioned by a success-oriented society and taught to be aggressive, but always within socially accepted bounds.

6. *Sexual restraint.*—Because of the Puritan value on sexual appropriateness, sexual intercourse was disapproved until after the marriage vows. Men restrained their sexual urges; copulation was a private function; prostitution was illegal; adultery was a basis for divorce; nudity was outlawed; rape was worthy of death and child-molestation was one of the worst crimes in society. Society prized sexual restraint and until recently vetoed sexual freedom. But now moviemakers put on the screen what was unthinkable, and "X" marks the spot. The sex-explosion has thumbed its nose at the Puritan ethic.

7. *Clean and correct language.*—Pure language is a crucial issue in today's public schools. "Can we enforce clean speech upon all children?" Some ask if we have the legal right to "muzzle children from using profanity in the schools." We have grown up in a society that valued

nonvulgar speech, but the pendulum seems to be swinging to the filthy side. Not only are children allowed to swear, they degrade other pupils and condemn teachers to damnation with little thought of their oath. There seems to be no saturation point for the superabundant display of vulgarity. Every conversation in high school seems to be an expression of the filth found on most bathroom walls. But most distressing is the fact that public school administrators use similar language in order to ingratiate themselves with the students.

Dirty Speech

At one time it was inappropriate to curse in front of ladies and children. Now small children use language that would blush the ears of a sailor. Whereas women were once placed on a pedestal, one high school teacher complains, " Girls are more vulgar than the boys."

Also, correct English was the earmark of an educated man. The exemplary person was able to communicate correctly and effectively. Schools no longer hold up the standard of proper English, but have dipped to the vernacular. The axiom seems to be "anything that will communicate," rather than observe the discipline of learning proper grammar.

8. *Moderation.*—The nation was built on moderation, especially where alcohol was concerned. Even though the Puritans disapproved of strong drink and we went through prohibition, drinking alcohol has been practiced since the birth of the nation. Since alcohol releases inhibitions and our ethic suppressed a full display of emotions, moderation was advocated.[7] When it came to clothing, recreation, and attitudes, moderation has been taught in our schools. Tennyson advocated,

Be not the first, by which the new is tried,
Be not the last, by which the old is laid aside.

Since there is definable truth, man should not deviate too far from its border. Therefore, society assumed that it could not go to the extremes of the religious-right, nor did man have the inner compulsion to drift to the left.

9. *Honesty.*—Bound up in economic values was religious doctrine. Since God required all things done properly, monetary matters reflected that value. Since God is related to money, it must be earned and spent honestly; proper records must be kept. Of course the Protestant ethic demanded honesty because religion demanded it. But in an economic community, honesty is necessary because it assures business prosperity. Credit is built on honesty. Without it society would degenerate into a barter system. If all people are honest and honor their obligation, then society prospers.

10. *Hard work and self-discipline.*—The Protestant ethic has prized diligent labor, knowing that it leads to success. Since success is a subconscious motivation, the means whereby men arrive at success is also valued. Max Weber analyzed the work ethic and concluded, "Labor must, on the contrary, be performed as if it were an absolute end in itself, a calling." [8] He noted that the Protestants veiwed daily work as a vocation of God. Man worked for more than money; he worked to please God. As a result, work took on a religious meaning, and Americans worked with religious devotion. They didn't work to gain salvation or work because of salvation; man worked because of its value within the Protestant ethic.

11. *Doing one's duty.*—The old cliché refuses to die: "If a job is worth doing, it is worth doing well." Duty had its own value and devotion was its self-reward. Be-

cause God established institutions, man placed value on his duty to them. Because man is responsible to God for his actions, man places value on his duty to obligation. Because success is an inner quality of life, man values duty as its own reward.

12. *Learning is its own reward.*—Deep down in the subconscious of Americans is a reverence for education. Many immigrants sacrificed so their sons could go to high school. The young daughter who graduated from college was the pride of a poor family. Getting all the education possible has been an American dream.

The Good Life

An ethic is no good unless it has a purpose. The Protestant ethic was the cohesive element of society and pointed man to "the good life." Whether "the good life" grew out of the Protestant ethic, or vice versa, is academic. The basic question involves a definition of "the good life." Those who came out of Europe, England, and other nations of the world immigrated to America seeking the best of all possible worlds. Many came for nonreligious reasons, seeking the life as it was found here. The good life was freedom from tyranny; man wanted freedom from the control of kings, church, slavery, ignorance and legal oppression. America's Statue of Liberty beckoned:

Give me your tired, your poor, your huddled masses yearning to breathe free. The wretched refuse from your teeming shore. Send these, the homeless, tempest-tossed, to me; I lift my lamp beside the golden door!

The good life was freedom: freedom from religion and freedom of religion: freedom from politics and freedom in politics; freedom from ignorance and freedom in education. The good life was free enterprises; a man could accumulate his millions or enjoy his warm cottage, both available within a man's ambition, talents, strength, and opportunity. The good life was available to all, and education was its foundation.

American Nightmare

But the American dream is being interrupted by threatening nightmares. The good life is now defined by existential self-meaning: a young man must find himself, express himself, and experience the satisfaction of the moment (hedonism). Today's good life revolts against discipline; young people seek a restrictionless society. Bombarded by advertisements, professional sports, and consumer-oriented society, young people are conscious of enjoyment of life as a basic reason for existence. The good life is the *Now* feeling. The day this book was finished, a neighborhood teen observed, "With Watergate, the energy crisis, pollution and war threatening in the Middle East, the golden age is over. I might as well drop out of college and do what I want."

Weber and the Protestant Ethic

The first person to describe the Protestant ethic was Max Weber in his outstanding volume, *The Protestant Ethic and the Spirit of Capitalism*. Weber attributes the success of the United States to the Protestant ethic. Writing as a German sociologist-philosopher, he has insight into the causes of American success not seen by others. His contributions cannot be ignored in this study. Weber describes the Protestant ethic as "the ownership of capital in management and the upper ranks of labor, in great modern industrial and commercial enterprises, may in part be explained in terms of historical circumstances . . . in which religious affiliation is not a cause of the economic conditions but to a certain extent appears to be a result of them." [9]

Weber claims the Protestant has a more intensive form of religious pride which penetrates and dominates his whole life. His religious seat of authority makes man responsible for both moral and social life. He examines the nations of Europe, noting that, "the Calvinistic *dispora* was the seedbed of capitalistic economy." [10] Here Weber found an evidence of economic growth and expansion. He sees strong development of business acumen as characteristic of revivalistic sectarian groups. Weber does not attribute financial success to the growth of the Enlightenment, "the spirit of hard work, of progress, or whatever else it may be called, the awakening of which one is inclined to ascribe to Protestantism." Here Weber found "a tendency to do, as joy of living, not found in any other sense, as connected with the Enlightenment." [11] Weber further attempts to define the Protestant ethic, "This term can be applied . . . to a complex of elements associated in historical reality which we unite into a conceptual whole from the standpoint of their cultural significance." [12]

Weber sees the growth of the Protestant ethic in four areas: (1) Calvinism in Western Europe; (2) Pietism; (3) Methodism; and (4) the sects growing out of the Baptistic movement. [13]

Weber praises the spirit of capitalism because it had to fight for its existence against a whole world of hostile forces. [14] The Protestant Reformation took place in the fringe nations of the Roman Catholic empire. Wealth was centered at the Vatican and France. Yet these fringe na-

tions have accumulated wealth while the Catholic nations have grown progressively poorer in comparison.

Weber deals with the question, "Why are the Catholics
not endued with the same ethic, inasmuch as their faith
comes from the same scriptural force, the Word of God?"
Growing out of this question is a second one, "Why do
Protestant nations enjoy a higher standard of living than
Catholic nations?" The difference is the expression of their
faith as evidenced in the outworking of salvation between
the two churches. The Protestant church teaches grace,
which places responsibility back upon its members for
proper living. The Catholic holds a sacerdotal system,
whereby man works for his salvation. The Catholic can
attend his church, confess his sins, and go away feeling a
sense of relief from guilt. Therefore, because he is for-
given, he is no longer responsible for his sins. The Protestant does not have the confessional booth. He is
responsible to live a holy life because he will have to give
an account to God at a future judgment. As a result, the
Protestant is more responsible for his actions.

Weber maintains that in the Catholic "works" system
man has immediate rewards that bring about immediate
responsibility but relieve him from future responsibility.
In reverse order, a value on the future is being built into
the Protestant because he will be judged in the future,
therefore he modifies his actions in the present. Since accountability is placed on the individual, he becomes responsible.

The average Catholic worker has often been portrayed
as the blue-collar worker. He works diligently for his
wages to provide shelter, clothing, food and the few nec-
essities of life; there is no further rationale for work. On
the other hand, the Protestant ethic leads to a work ethic.

The Protestant works because he is responsible to God; he is working to please God. Many American business-men have found themselves compulsively chained to their job, working more than the 9:00 to 5:00 routine. They stay on the job because work is their existential concept of self-identity.

Weber sees another contrast between the Catholic and Protestant ethic, dealing with man's ultimate expression of obedience to God. The Catholics taught that man's ultimate calling was to subdue his worldly desires in mo-nastic asceticism. Thomas Aquinas taught that activity in the world is a thing of the flesh, even though willed by God. The ultimate path to please God was to withdraw into the monastery and separate oneself from the world. Martin Luther taught that labor was a calling by God and an outward expression of one's faith. The Protestant taught that the individual was to remain at the station in which God had called him and to restrain his worldly activities within the limit imposed by that established station. Weber explains "that work is the calling by God," rather than a task to earn money. The Protestant ethic that grew out of Luther's teaching stated that the fulfill-ment of worldly duties is the only way to live acceptably to God. Work is the will of God for all men. Weber feels the moral justification of work was one of the most impor-tant outward results of the Reformation.[15]

As a result, Weber sees a different mentality among Catholics than among Protestants. He states, "The Cath-olic . . . having less of the asquisitive impulse, prefers a life of the greatest possible security, even with a smaller income, to a life of risk and excitement, even though it may bring the chance of gaining honor and riches." [16]

However, in Weber's theory he found that the opportunity of earning more money was not as attractive as working less. By this he maintains "Man does not by nature wish to earn more money, but simply to live as he is accustomed to live and to earn as much as is necessary for that purpose." [17] As a result, Weber sees that a man's attitude rather than financial incentive determines how he works. Therefore, if attitude is more important than financial return, the Protestant ethic will produce more work than will the promise of more money.

Weber sees the Protestants' desire for success growing because they live in nations where they are excluded from positions of political influence; hence, "Their aimless members seek to satisfy the desire for recognition of their abilities in economic zeal, since there is no opportunity in the service of the state." [18] Weber feels that the *suma bonum* of the Protestant ethic is earning more and more money combined with the strict avoidance of all spontaneous enjoyment of life. Many Protestants would disagree, seeing this as the result of their faith, whereas Weber implies it is the aim of their faith. Whether cause or effect, he felt Protestants accumulated money because of a future ethic. As a result, Weber sees man as dominated by making and acquiring more money as the ultimate purpose of his life.[19]

Wall Street Needs Protestants

Many feel democracy is based on man's selfish interests of making money. When the Protestant work ethic is removed, democracy will continue. However, democracy as we know it in America can collapse because the Protestant/Puritan ethic is removed. Weber indicates, "As every employer knows, the lack of conscience by the laborers of such countries—for instance Italy as compared with Germany—has been, and to a certain percent still is, one of the principle obstacles to a capitalistic development." Weber startles us all by indicating, "The difference does not lie in the degree of development of any impulse to make money . . ." [20] The difference lies in the ethic which holds society together.

Weber felt that the business life in the small frontier communities of the United States would have fallen into the barter system were it not for the Protestant ethic, which placed value on banking money for the future, valuing money as an adornment of God and conducting business in an exact manner which he describes as "the essence of moral conduct . . . commanded in the name of duty." [21] So he sees Protestantism developing, "an individualistic capitalistic economy . . . directed with foresight and caution toward success which is in sharp contrast to the hand-to-mouth existence of the peasant and the privileged traditionalism of the skilled craftsman of Europe." [22]

The catalyst of our nation is changing. The traditional Protestant/Puritan ethic was the subconscious value that holds nations, social groups, and subcultures in a harmonious working relationship. The Protestant/Puritan ethic is like mortar holding the brick building together. The superstructure is only as strong as the cohesiveness of new mortar.

Society's ethic is like a monetary system. Paper money has no value in itself, and is respected only because of common agreement as to its worth. If everyone valued currency according to his own desire, no one would know the worth of the dollar he holds in his hand. When society's ethic is valued differently by everyone, it has no value. In other words, an ethic is not an autonomous value, but a medium of exchange. The basis of freedom is common values to give meaning to our actions. When a society has no basis of agreement, it begins to die. If education does not serve the values of society, it accentuates the deterioration process.

Many applaud the advent of the post-Christian ethic, but are they prepared for the post-American area?

NOTES

1. As much as I believe in proper biblical indoctrination, it belongs in the church school, not in the public school.

2. Robert J. Havinghurst, "Human Development, Societal Change and Adult Moral Character," *Religious Education,* LXVIII (May-June 1973), p. 408.

3. Robert J. Havinghurst, Bernice Neugarten, *Society and Education* (Boston: Allyn and Bacon, Inc., 1962), p. 150, 151.

4. Willard Waller, *The Sociology of Teaching* (New York: John Wiley and Sons, 1932), p. 103.

5. Havinghurst and Neugarten, p. 74.

6. Max Weber, *The Protestant Ethic and the Spirit of Capitalism,* trans. Talcott Parsons (New York: Charles Scribners Sons, 1958). The concept of the Protestant ethic is presented on pp. 1-74.

7. The Author feels the New Testament teaches abstinence, even though the Protestant ethic allows for moderation.

8. Weber, p. 62.

9. *Ibid.,* p. 35, 36. An extensive analysis is made of Weber's thesis regarding the Protestant ethic. He is considered the authority in this study and all works on this topic still refer to his monumental contribution.

10. *Ibid.,* p. 43.

11. *Ibid.,* p. 44, 45.

12. *Ibid.,* p. 47.

13. *Ibid.*, p. 95.
14. *Ibid.*, p. 56.
15. *Ibid.*, p. 85.
16. *Ibid.*, p. 41.
17. *Ibid.*, p. 60.
18. *Ibid.*, p. 36.
19. *Ibid.*, p. 53.
20. *Ibid.*, p. 57.
21. *Ibid.*, p. 75.
22. *Ibid.*, p. 76.

8 A Prod to The Public Schools

Sending every child to a Christian school is not the answer to the problems of the public schools. Even though some Protestant ministers might want every American child in a Christian school, this is unrealistic. I am committed to the Christian school and believe that strong Christian schools are the hope for America; yet I do not want to see the public schools destroyed. They are synonymous with freedom. America needs a vibrant public school system to communicate our historical past and thus insure a stable future. The public school should be committed to truth, academic excellence, the American way of life, free enterprise, rugged individualism and decency. Every American still has the right to life, liberty, and the pursuit of happiness.

As the public school dips its colors, the Christian school movement carries on the cause. History shows Christianity has always triumphed in the cause of freedom and truth (John 1:9, 8:12,32–36). If the Christian school movement is going to make a vital contribution to the United States, it must be free. We should not make Christian schools conform to the failures of the public schools. Laws are now being passed to require Christian school teachers to meet state certification. Further, laws are being pushed on Christian schools regarding sizes of rooms, class load, and course requirements. One state even requires two flag poles for state certification, then requires certification for a private school to exist. Must the process of education require two flag poles for existence?

American life is described as post-Christian; the Protestant–Puritan ethic is gone, and church attendance is declining.[1] Just as the Catholic church once built parochial schools to perpetuate its existence in America, Protestant churches need Protestant schools. But the life style in our nation is also post-American. We have lost our sense of spiritual unity and purpose. A strong Christian school will improve the public schools, champion the cause of freedom, and reinforce the American value system. The Christian school movement can make the following contributions to our nation in its post-Christian/post-American area.

Christian Schools

1. *The Christian schools are a standard.* With the academic deterioration in the public schools, the Christian schools are dedicated to answering the question, "Why can't Johnny read?" Much rhetoric is heard on "Reading, 'Riting and 'Rithmetic." Thus far, most Christian schools administer the same proficiency test as their neighboring public schools. Usually, the Christian schools score higher, and their principals come out cheering. But public school educators are defensive. They point out that the better student is usually taken out of public school and registered in private institutions; naturally, they would score higher on achievement tests. Second, students from affluent families, who traditionally scored higher on IQ examinations, tend to go to private schools. Therefore, it

is only natural that pupils from private schools would score higher on achievement tests. Third, concerned parents traditionally have supervised pupil homework and supported school activities. Therefore, we could only expect higher scores from students of private schools than those of public schools. Even though public school educators claim the private schools score higher because better students attend, they also claim in the same breath that their education is comparable. This is a smoke screen and makes as much sense as saying the rich are wealthier than the poor because they have more money. The issue is academic excellence. Who has the best results? The private schools have superior students who score better on achievement tests than those in the public schools. Therefore, their performance will be an academic standard to public schools.

2. *Christian schools are a conscience.*—Webster defines the conscience, "The internal recognition of right and wrong as regarding one's actions and motives." Conscience is the *process* of internal recognition, not the *cause,* i.e. a moral regulator. The American conscience recognizes the basic right of the individual. It stems from the Protestant/Puritan ethic which elevated man because he was made in the image of God. An abuse of man's dignity is considered wrong. The Christian schools adhere to the American conscience in principle and attempt to implement it in practice. As the Christian school adheres to the moral worth of every person, it will judge those who abuse that principle. The Christian school stands for liberty, dignity and rugged individualism. This does not mean all public schools have deviated from this standard nor does it indicate all Christian schools are righteous. Pure conscience does not automatically guarantee pure

living. It provides an internal recognition of right and wrong. Therefore the Christian school will motivate all society to a higher moral law.

3. *The Christian school is the leaven of society.*—Paul spoke about the need for leaven (1 Cor. 5:6), which permeated the whole lump, no part was left untouched. As committed Christians graduate from the Christian schools, they enter every area of life. Not all products from Christian schols will act Christian, but the influence of those who do cannot be ignored. Whereas the average American makes his investment to society out of respect to the nation, the Christian has greater loyalty to God. He senses a responsibility for consistent living, devotion to God, loyalty to institutions, dedication to his employment, and fairness to his fellow men. Hence, the Christian will be a better American citizen.

Evangelism

If Christians are conscientious in their faith, they will attempt to win others to Jesus Christ (Acts 1:8), and teach them Christianity (Matt. 28:20). Their evangelistic endeavors will have a leavening effect on society, because as they attempt to make others Christian, they will be making them better Americans.

4. *A Christian school upholds freedom.*—The American society was built on conformity to the whole, yet recognizes the uniqueness of subcultures. Freedom of religion is a basic plank in the American platform. Every individual has the right to freedom of religion with the unique practices of his faith. The freedom of a large section of the American public is threatened. Do the parents in churches have the right to educate their children according to the demands of their faith? This volume raises the

question, "Does the nation determine what shall be taught our children, or does the church have the right to instruct its young?" Many Christian churches and schools feel their freedom of religion is threatened. States are requiring certification from accredited institutions, yet some four year colleges with outstanding departments of education refuse accreditation because the college rejects external control. Should the church school which believes in freedom from state control in education, have the right to choose teachers who believe in freedom from state control in certification? If the answer is *no,* our nation has had it.

Threats to Freedom

Building codes, inspectors, local ordinances, and state licensing are all threats to religious freedom. In many instances, local ordinances require the Christian school to conform to the norms of public schools. When asked who determined the size for schoolrooms, the answer invariably comes back, "The public school." But the inevitable question is asked, "Should the Christian school, which believes the public schools have failed, be required to meet the ordinances which led to their failure? If the answer is "*Yes,*" then our nation has had it.

5. *A Christian school is prophetic.* In the Old Testament, the prophet was the spokesman for God. He was called the seer (1 Samuel 9:9). Being the eyes for God, he saw imminent judgment and called the nation to repentance. A study of the Scriptures reveals that the prophetic office was most evident when the nation drifted from God. Most Christians would not send their children to private schools if the public schools were doing their job. The growing phenomena of the Christian schools is a

prophetic voice against the public shcools, repeating the warning, "Public schols have failed." The composite desire of those in Christian schools is for public schools to return to their priorities.

Do Christian Schools Have a Future?

I would hope that the Christian school movement would become no longer necessary because the public schools returned to their original priorities. Then we parents who pay double for education could safely enroll our children in the local school. But my voice is only one against the opinion of teachers, administrators, and numberless others who are committed to the present drift of public education.

Since I don't expect much change in the public schools, my hope lies with Christian schools. They will grow in number and size. They will continue to be established by conservative churches, not liberal Christianity, which is synonymous with secular humanism. Why should churches holding liberal theology build private schools? The public schools already propagate the liberalisms held by many mainline denominations. Conservative churches must educate to survive, just as early Catholic immigrants felt they had to establish parochial schools to survive.

But there are ominous clouds on the horizon. They threaten the otherwise bright future of Christian schools. The public school already is mounting a counterattack. Protestant churches see the militancy as an attack on their religious liberty. Public schools claim they want all private schools to meet their standards. These battles will only intensify a desire by Christians to educate their children according to their life-style. Therefore:

Every concerned citizen should raise a protest against the abuses of public school education.

Every conservative church ought to consider the possibility of establishing a Christian school.

Every Christian parent ought to enroll his children in a Christian school.

NOTES

1. Elmer Towns, *Is The Day Of The Denomination Dead?* (Nashville: Thomas Nelson, Inc. 1973). Chapter two examines the statistics of church decline and suggests reasons for the downward trend.

9 Solution: A Return From Liberalism

Stopped at a red light on a main boulevard in a Midwestern city with a pastor, I pointed out a crumpled looking high school girl thumbing a ride in the opposite direction.

Her dejected thumb was uninviting, and the dazed eyes showed complete unconcern for the world around her. She wore muddy, dragging jeans. If she had on shoes, I couldn't tell. I couldn't see her feet. The matted pullover sweater with pulled threads was stretched out of shape. The hardened splotches appeared to be crusted food or blood. Her long hair was snarled and frizzy.

"Giving her a ride is about as inviting as carrying garbage to the dump," I casually mentioned to my pastor-companion.

"That's the Smith girl," my front seat companion noted. The parents had once attended his church. Unfolding a gruesome tale, he told how the girl's parents had given her flute lessons, ballet, and always enrolled her in the finest summer camps. "Mrs. Smith is a meticulous housekeeper, and Mr. Smith has always been careful about his appearance. He sells insurance." The pastor remembered the family, explaining they were a typical American family. "The children have never been spanked because the mother is a disciple of Dr. Spock," he explained. The mother had come to the preacher for counseling about the girl.

He quickly enumerated what the mother told him. The girl became active in the student protest movement, was involved in a sit-down strike in the school halls. On one occasion several fellows brought her home drunk at 3 A.M. She ran away from home for a week, finally calling from Chicago for her parents to come get her. "The mother thought she had done everything possible for her daughter," the preacher-counselor concluded.

Rage settled over my thoughts. "Who ruined the girl?" I silently asked.

Our conversation touched several sources that influence kids, i.e. television, movies, rock music, mobility, and affluence. Finally, we agreed that the public schools have a deeper influence on most students and a wider influence on all students.

Pubilc school ruins kids. Their educators bristle at this charge. Yet, their educators smile approvingly when someone maintains public schools have been the greatest influence on children, making America the greatest nation on the face of the earth.

More and more Americans are disgusted at the products of the public school. Some are irritated because the American way of life is changing. Others are disgusted at the waste of their tax money. But many are threatened by its influence on their children. Not all public schools are guilty of every charge hurled against them. Some public schools like some judges are constitutionalists in purpose: they still serve the community. There are some good public schools. However, the evidences of cancer are in the system, long before the symptoms of dreaded disease are discovered. The school where your children attend may appear satisfactory at present, but parents should guard for signs of deterioration.

These following suggestions involve correcting the public school's destiny. These are not suggestions for day-to-day operation. If practical suggestions for minute changes were made, an operational handbook for public school education would have to be writen covering every minor aspect of school administration. The purpose here is to point out crucial areas where a change in policy would affect the overall direction of public schools. When this is done, minor details will take care of themselves.

1. *Recognition that parents are responsible for the health, education, and welfare of their children.*—The basic framework of laws in the United States recognizes that a child is not responsible until the legal age of eighteen. Historically, parents have been responsible for the crimes of their young, juvenile judges have released offenders into the custody of their parents. There is a legal battle brewing over the educational stewardship of children. Is the public school responsible for them? Historically, the parent has been responsible. (See chapters 5 and 6) The historical precedent and Biblical mandate demand that parents be responsible for their children. Parents give birth to children. Parents pay school taxes. Parents vote on bond issues. Parents elect lawmakers. Parents are the United States Government.

2. *Schools must remain public rather than becoming government schools.*—There is an ideological fight for possession of the public schools. The National Education Association (NEA) wants to control our schools. Federal judges want to use our schools to correct social injustice. Educational bureaucrats want to fashion the school into their concept of education. Even students want to control

our schools. Children who have no concept of history nor present understanding of the United States, would weaken the public school into a sociological playground, twisting their education into selfish pursuits. No one aspect of society should control the public schools. They belong to the public and serve society. Just as a recent Supreme Court ruling on pornography allowed community standards to decide decency, so the public school should conform itself to community standard, each locality sharing its voice in the public schools.

3. *Public schools should assume their fair share of responsibility for the failures of society.*—The educators have been super-defensive about criticism. When their shortcomings are pointed out, educators are quick to shed responsibility, claiming, "We only mirror society, our failures come from the community." The public schools are charged with the education of children and anything less than an adequate job is a failure.

4. *Recognition and communication of the values of the United States.*—The Protestant/Puritan ethic is the catalyst for business, society, and government. This has been the American ethic. It is the basis on which our society has operated. The public school has been the main "carrier" of the American ethic. Since hard work has built our nation, public schools should teach our children to work. Since honesty is the foundation of a society built on credit cards, checking, and business agreement, public schools should punish cheating and lying. (See chapter 7) The public schools must recognize the American values, then communicate them so our children can enjoy the freedom we have experienced.

5. *Public schools should not be operated on the level of the lowest complaints.*—One of the main foundation

of democracy is, "Let the minority have their say, let the majority have their way." The public schools should never be controlled by a small faction which criticizes its policy. Strong institutions function according to policy. Weak institutions make policy in view of critics. Small hard-core revolutionary groups have shut down colleges. The same has happened in high schools, forcing principals to send all students home. Spineless administrators are guilty of social injustices bowing to the expediency of the moment. Being pressured by the presence of TV cameras or the threat of suit by the ACLU, school administrators have not defended justice for the majority. The school is like water seeking its own level, when standards are watered down, the whole school puddles to the lowest level.

6. *A recognition of the nature of the pupil.*—The naïve liberal maintains that the child is only good. The hard-headed Calvinist maintains that man is only evil. Between these two extremes lies a path for the public schools. The naïve liberal is wrong, the child has destructive forces. Let the egg-headed humanist look through his rosy glasses at the multimillion dollar loss in broken school windows. Let him interview young girls who have been raped on school facilities. Let him hear the filth spewed out by vindictive teens at their teachers. Let him observe callous students who refuse to take advantage of the greatest educational opportunity ever afforded. The pupil has internal tendencies which will destroy himself and his society. The public school must incorporate into its thinking the fact that any pupil is capable of committing atrocities, like the shocking newspaper headlines. Those who originated the Constitution framed laws to protect man from himself.

Not only must educators deal with pupils in light of

their destructive tendencies, education must do all it can to overcome man's animal nature. This does not mean man's destructive forces can be eradicated in any one individual, nor can the be eliminated from society. But a recognition of man's destructive forces will help educators to deal with life as it is.

On the other side of the coin, every student has unlimited constructive forces, greater than any teacher in his glowing optimism could expect from any child. Walk through the art classes and see objects of beauty, created by students. Listen to the average student council discuss ways to correct social injustice. Watch student teams clean up river banks, work with retarded children or collect money for the Red Cross. Students have positive contributions to make to the world of engineering. Their irate condemnation of Watergate does not always arise from antiestablishment tendencies. They have a consuming desire for decency in government. The student is an enigma: he is capable of both good and evil. With a Jekyll/Hyde personality, he responds to the strongest voice and follows the convincing guide. Therefore, the public school must recognize both tendencies in pupils and draw out the positive nature.

But the public schools must do more than recognize the dual nature of the pupil. They should make pupils aware of their own nature. Every student should realize his destructive forces as well as the good he can accomplish. Those who don't properly understand themselves, can't live a full life. The unexamined life is not worth living.

7. *The public schools should be consistent with their total-life philosophy of education.*—Colonial schools claimed only to educate the mind. Gradually the public schools evolved into a socialization process, concerning

themselves with preparing the total man with total living. This sounds great in principle, but public schools deny it in practice. The schools seem to ignore attitudes of culture and deportment. At one time, schools concerned themselves with the dress code of students, attempting to lift their standards of cleanliness and appropriateness; developing personal habits of decency. With the influx of the hippie-revolution, standards for cleanliness have been thrown out. Principals no longer require young boys to have styled clean hair (the current fashion). A young girl can wear to school whatever her mother chooses. Instead of lifting each pupil to the standard set by the school, administrators have dropped standards to the dirtiest level of the one student who refuses to wash. Hence, they are inconsistent with their total man philosophy of education. Once public schools were the "carrier" of patriotism, but when pupils protest saluting the flag, it is quietly dropped from home-room exercises.

8. *The public schools should not be used as political instruments to solve social problems.* The majority of Americans agree that every student, regardless of race, should have equal opportunities, under the law. But racial inequity still abounds. No one who adheres to the Constitution condones racial injustice. Many have thought that forced busing would solve racial inequities, but our schools grow weaker rather than better. Student achievement on tests plummets. The Coleman Reports indicate the family, not the school, is the center of inequities. It was thought that when children grow up together, racial distinctives would be minimized. Yet forced busing has brought to the surface deep racial hatred that was thought nonexistent in Northern cities. Forced busing has not brought harmony to Southern cities. Now the black com-

munities, for whom forced busing was instigated, are developing respect for black culture. Although its principle grows yearly, "Black is beautiful," the cliché, is no longer heard.

There Are Other Ways

Our children are too important to be used as an experiment. Our schools have been too influential to become guinea pigs for social innovators. Let the schools educate. There are other ways to solve the problems of racial injustice.

9. *Stop giving the public schools a messianic role.*— Americans have long considered education as the panacea for all ills. Therefore we devise vocational schools, driver education, sex education, narcotic education, community-relations seminars, and any other courses to solve the latest problem in the newspaper. Schools have been given a messianic character, and to a certain degree, they have been instrumental in American ingenuity. We believe any problem can be solved. We also realize that education is effective—it can change society. But as the curriculum is broadened, academic requirements are watered down. Educational perspectives change. So let's stop using schools for noneducational purposes. Johnny still can't read as well as he used to. But the more distressing question: Is Johnny losing his *desire* to read?

10. *Revise the compulsory attendance laws for education.*—One of the most important legal enactments was the universal education law. Americans guaranteed national greatness by requiring every citizen to be educated. The basic assumption of Christianity is that light dispels darkness, and knowledge guarantees progress.

Universal education laws were necessary in their day,

but times have changed. Public schools no longer guarantee freedom: they are becoming government schools. Individuality is lost as conformity to the state grows. The growth of the Christian school will insure freedom and individualism.

The laws regarding compulsory public school attendance should allow parents to choose an education for their children. But the critics complain that quality would suffer. A guarantee for an educated citizenry could be a national testing program at the end of each year in high school (a system currently used in Canada, England, France). Students in the Christian school would have the freedom of education, yet their education could be compared with that of public school graduates. This is only an illustration of solving the problem, not a suggestion for educational policy. Compulsory attendance at public schools by all school age children, ruling out attendance at a Christian school, could eventually destroy American liberty.

11. *Business needs a larger voice in public schools.*— The business community bears a large brunt of taxation. It also employs a majority of the graduates from public school. The business and manufacturing community have a large stake in the nature and future of the American society. Since the public school is the "carrier" of that culture, they should have a voice in its affairs.

12. *Re-examine the role of discipline in education.*—In 1958 Sputnik accomplished something that all of the rhetoric of Admiral Rickover could not. The Russian success forcibly moved American education into an accelerated space-science effort. Apparently the public schools followed a drift in emphasis from hard-core to the soft-fringe. The word "education" still means "to control," and the process of education should result in discipline, affect-

ting a student's thinking, acting and feeling. The student should be controlled by truth, and reciprocally, control the light to which he has been exposed. When educators allow students to "do their own thing" pupils miss the world "out there."

But the public schools should not revert to a spartanic atmosphere, where educational control turns into slavery. True education is sensitive to pupils but it also gives allegiance to objective truth. Discipline is needed in every area of school; academic, physical, social, sexual, psychological; expressed in students' habits and attitudes.

13. *Allow creationism to be taught as one explanation for the cause of the world.*—For approximately 200 years public school textbooks taught that the world was created by God. Beginning in 1859 the theory of evolution began spreading, after Charles Darwin published *The Origin of The Species.* Since that time, liberal Christianity has incorporated evolution into its doctrinal statement, because it allows for faith without belief in the supernatural. The public school textbooks have incorporated evolution and taught it as fact, when it remains a theory, as yet unproved.

This manuscript does not ask the public schools to teach supernatural creationism to explain the origin of the universe. Many Christians would be satisfied if creationism requires textbooks to include creationism.
were taught as one of the explanations. California law now
14. *Stop the spread of unionism among public schools.* —Labor unions have made a vital contribution to the American society and have contributed to its financial prosperity. The establishment of unions has stopped the perpetration of economic injustice on workers, given job security, stabilized the economy and assured that the best

workers get the top dollar. *Unionism* is the abuse by labor unions, permitting featherbedding, and pawning off shoddy work under the security of "you can't fire me." Unionism allows labor leaders to invade the realm of management, it destroys the dichotomy of labor and management.

First, a serious question should be raised if public school teachers should be unionized. Teaching is a humanitarian endeavor; it is not part of the free-enterprise business world. There are no profits to share, nor is there a competitor to whom the employee can go for work. When they strike for higher wages, teachers are borrowing from the future of the public schools. Their salaries come out of tax money and there is only so much available.

Second, teacher unions are seeking a larger voice in educational policy. They should make contributions to the process, teachers are considered professionals, not common laborers. But the schools belong to the public, schools do not belong to teachers. The following definition of a schoolteacher has far-reaching shock waves.

A schoolteacher is the extension of the parent's responsibility to society for preparing the pupil to live in the culture in which the school exists.

Note the implication of the above definition. First, everything the parent is to the child, the public school teacher is to his class. This involves example, leadership, concern and love. Second, the schoolteacher is responsible to pass on the society in which he lives. Total heritage is important. Third, the teacher has an accountability to parents and society. He does not own, nor should he seek to control, the public schools. The teacher makes his contribution to the pupil in light of his accountability to society.

15. *Call a national conference on educational aims.*— The public schools need to take a hard look at themselves and ask difficult questions. The aims of public school need to be re-examined in light of national needs, priorities and objectives. I feel the public school is floating aimlessly in a drifting society. The problems facing the public school need to be defined. The basic nature of education needs to be redefined, including an examination of its contribution to society, detailing its limitation and excesses. Only when a majority of those involved in education realize needs, diagnosis, prescription and therapy, can anything be done about our schools.

Is There a Solution?

This volume would not be realistic if it suggested all students enroll in Christian schools. This volume would not be pro-American if it applauded the death of public schools. This volume would not be ethical if it did not suggest ways to "save" our public schools.

This chapter suggests basic changes in the philosophic direction of our schools. There is little any one individual can do regarding these 15 items. (Over 50 practical suggestions are made in chapter 10). These suggestions will speak to some in the educational community. My wife and secretary typed this volume. They kept reminding me of their failure to change the public school where their children used to attend. But just as every farmer sows in hope and a child is conceived in expectation, this author offers his suggestions for a restoration and renewal of the public schools. The solution is a return from liberalism.

10 How Can You Change Your Public School?

"I can't afford to send my children to a private school," complained Rosann Reuther in an editorial meeting after reading this manuscript. She is an account executive with Holder and Kennedy, Nashville, an advertising agency.

"This is a great book, but it needs one more chapter . . . you've got to tell me how to improve the public school around the corner."

Rosann is a typical working mother, in her middle twenties. She is a part of the American way of life. With a desperate look in her eye, she said, "I want my children to turn out right." Rosann and her husband had looked into a private school but were unable to enroll their little boy there. They felt locked into the public school around the corner.

I immediately began asking adults how they could change the public schools. Some parents had no practical idea of how to change their public schools, even though they had strong opinions. Parents are like Don Quixote charging windmills. After I left the advertising agency, a middle-aged, balding salesman from a small town in Indiana sat next to me on the plane and confessed, "Ten years ago we had one school in our community, and I was satisfied with it . . . but not now." He wrinkled his forehead and analyzed, "There is no dedication among teachers today." When asked what is wrong with our schools, the smiling salesman declared that teachers get too much money. "Keep 'em poor and you'll keep 'em working." He admitted being a steward at a Methodist church and "keeping 'em poor" was their way of handling their pastor. Upon further analysis, he admitted poorly paid pastors had killed his church.

A young Jewish vice-president for a motel chain sat next to me on the following flight and was militant about changing the school. "Do away with tenure!" he demanded with a raised voice, protesting a system that allowed ineffective teachers to stay on forever.

"Teach foreign languages in the first grades." The obviously well-educated executive indicated he had learned Hebrew at the synagogue school. I pointed out to him that many adults want to project the type of education they had on to present day public schools. "No!" He reasoned that children should study hardest when their minds have the greatest power to absorb. He was in favor of Sesame Street, the Head Start program, and educational toys for children.

His four-year-old boy would never set foot in a public school, he claimed.

There are eight general areas whereby a parent can change the public school: (1) Beginning at home, a parent can positively reinforce the kind of education he wants for his child, or negatively counteract the public school influence. (2) By relating to the Board of Education, a parent can make constructive suggestions or voice his disagreement with policies. (3) Parents can communicate to the school administration the kind of education he desires for his child. (4) Each parent can relate with his child's classroom teacher, sharing aspirations and expectations for the child. The home and teacher can support one another in their educational endeavors. (5) The media as an avenue of change have been primarily used by counter-revolutionaries. Now that our public schools are threatened, parents can use media to voice their disagreement with the public schools. (6) America has a number of supportive institutions with vital interest in the public schools. The parent will find aid for his concern in his PTA, local church, civic clubs, business community, and other institutions of society. (7) The legislative community is concerned both about criticism of public schools and the opinion of their clientele. Most legislators give attention to issues concerning a majority of their voters. Enroll their support. (8) Enrolling your child in a private school is both a first and last resort to change the public school. When enough parents take their children out of public schools, educators will sit up and take notice. Boycotting a business usually gets results. So does a strike when workers withhold their service. If you withhold your children from the public school, it will demand changes.

Set Your Own House in Order

Too many parents have tried to get somebody else to do their job. They want the public schools to educate their children, the Boy Scouts to instill character, the Department of Recreation to entertain them and the church to get them ready for heaven. A family needs all of these institutions to help rear its children, but remember, these institutions are only the extension of family influence into the life of the child. Where parents guide children in their homework, the school has an easier time communicating its lessons. When the home enforces cleanliness, loyalty and respect of individuals, the Boy Scouts are more effective in communicating character. Where the home conducts a family altar, the church will be more effective in teaching Christianity.

1. *Hold up the virtues of education.* Our children are familiar with the criticisms against the public schools. As they hear more and more complaints against their school, their respect for schools decreases. Don't let your child confuse education and schools. Parents must be sure their children do not look down on education because of criticism about the local public school. Even though one teacher may be bad does not mean your child should reject education. You want your child educated. Keep the goal of education before him. In spite of all the criticism they hear about schools, keep reminding your child that education brings progress and with it a better quality of living.

2. *Don't undermine the authority of the public school.* School leaders have earned their place in society. They fulfill useful functions. Don't belittle the principal or other public school administrators. Their judgment will not always be right because they are human. The inequities of administrators does not give your child the right to break school rules. Expect your child to submit to their authority. Teach your child it is never right, to do wrong, in order to establish right. Your child never has the right to break school rules, even when you and he disagree with the rule. If you feel a rule is undemocratic, work to get it changed.

Respect School Officials

Also, your child should respect school officials because of their office. Even when you disagree with the private opinion of administrators or disapprove of their personality, your child should show respect to an administrator's position.

3. *Support school discipline.* Most school administrators agree their biggest headache is parents who take sides with their children. Mr. J. R. Reynolds, principal of Herschel V. Jenkins High School in Savannah, Georgia, indicated many parents will not approach a conference with an open mind. "My child said . . ." is hurled at administrators by parents who won't listen to teachers. Therefore, when the public school corrects your child, don't immediately jump to his defense. Get facts before you get your fur up. When your child is wrong, and is punished, support the school.

4. *Don't protect your child to save your ego.* Many children are the extension of the parents' ego. Therefore, a mother becomes defensive regarding her child, interpreting any failure as a personal defeat. When the school office phones to check up on a student's absence, the parents will cover for the child rather than admit that he is cutting school. Of course, there are many other psychological adjustments why parents defend their children but instead of strengthening character, they weaken it by "defensive protectiveness."

It's Up to You

5. *See that your child is in school.* According to many administrators, absenteeism is the biggest discipline problem in the modern school. One principal indicated, "The doctors can't all be that busy on Friday afternoon," indicating he gets a multitude of excuse slips that children are going to the doctors on the last afternoon of each week. If school is important, your child should be there unless a reason arises more important than your child's

education and character. There is not much more important than that.

6. *Begin early to reinforce your subculture.* Give careful attention to the playmates of your child. As he begins playing with children of a different value system, educate him concerning your family values. Point out why you think cursing or nasty language is inappropriate. Discuss differences you see in other children with your child. Your child will become enriched in his outlook by playing with those of different subculture. However, when you sense an adverse influence on your child from someone of a different subculture, prohibit him from playing with that child.

7. *Teach your child to recognize subculture clashes.* Explain to him why he is different. Point out the differences in other children. Teach your child to respect others while building self respect. As an illustration start early and reinforce a clothing habit so that the child will respect cleanliness, appropriateness and culture.

8. *Tell your child not to believe everything he hears in school.* America is no longer a monolithic nation, it is a pluralistic society. The public school no longer stands for the traditional American ethic. Many of the values you hold are denied at school. Since we can no longer expect the public schools to support the American ethic, you must reinforce these beliefs in your child.

The Board of Education

Many feel the Board of Education is the most powerful instrument to influence the public schools. (Some disagree and indicate federal judges or legislators have more influence.) A parent should apply the following principles to work with the Board to improve the public schools:

(1) *Work to get conservatives elected on the school board.* Dr. Greg Dixon, Pastor of Indianapolis, Indiana, Temple where 600 students attend Baptist High School, indicates the major problem with public schools is liberalism in the Board of Education. Dixon maintains, "Every Christian ought to support conservative board members." Then the pastor reiterated, "Cut off federal control."

(2) *Attend meetings of the Board of Education.* An enlightened public will strengthen the public schools. Find out what's going on in your schools. Your concern will "prod" board members to a higher responsibility to the public.

(3) *Don't be afraid to go to the Board with your problems.* A parent should not run to the Board of Education with minor complaints. A chain of command is established and a parent begins with a classroom teacher, second he takes his problem to the school principal, next the superintendent of schools is consulted, and if no satisfaction is gotten, he should go to the Board of Education.

(4) *Examine carefully all school bond issues.* One of the best tools to express your democratic right is the ballot box. Vote only for those items you approve. If you don't understand any local referendum, phone local school authorities for an explanation.

(5) *Vote against fringe items to the education purpose of the school.* As public schools demand more and more money, parents have backed their financial demands. But now there is a growing resentment in the public to voting more money for public education. At times, failure of public school referendums has hurt children, especially where classes meet in the hallways or class size spirals out of proportion. As we see the proliferation of fringe services, one gets the impression that public schools are

more concerned with facilities than function. One gets the impression that equipment is more important than what goes on inside. Let your public school administrators know you will vote against elaborate counseling facilities, paved driver education courses for practice driving, special locker rooms for football teams, extensive music facilities, and theaters for drama and arts.

(6) *Inform the Board of Education of your opinion on education.* Be careful of irritating them with your minor gripes. Communicate to them your desire of items that will have a long range impact on public schools. Let them know your opinions on the following: (a) standards for the selection of new teachers; (b) an educational attitude toward discipline; (c) that the Board of Education should support administrative decisions; (d) allowing the teaching of a Christian interpretation of the universe along with the theory of evolution; (e) allowing the Christian heritage of the United States to be included in the public school curriculum (this is not the same as religious indoctrination).

7. *Encourage the Board of Education to be steadfast in their public trust.* Since the Board of Education has much to say about the direction of public schools, encourage them to resist encroachment on their authority from teacher unions, federalism and bureaucracy. Teacher unions are trying to take control of the schools away from the Board of Education. Federal aid to education has strings attached that usually tie the local schools to Washington. Bureaucrats tend to make decisions that should be decided at Board level. Encourage the Board of Education members to be faithful to their responsibility.

8. *Oppose teacher tenure.* Teachers have been striving for professional status with all of its advantages. How-

ever, a professional usually doesn't have job security. A doctor's patients or a lawyer's clients continue to use his services because of his competency. We never hear professionals clamor for job security. But teachers are ambivalent. They want the status of professionalism, yet the job security of blue collar workers. Unlimited tenure is supposed to protect academic freedom, but it protects teachers who don't grow professionally. It steals teacher incentive and initiative.

The Local School Administration

The Board of Education determines additional policy, administrators carry it out. Therefore a parent contacts the Board of Education to change policy; they approach local school administrators when policy is not being correctly administered.

(1) *Inform the school authorities of your desire for your child.* This can be done through a letter or a personal conference with school officials. Public school educators work for you, they are supported by your tax dollar. Educators should operate with a view of meeting public needs. In the role of public servants, they can provide service only according to public opinion. I have such great faith in public schools that if they knew community opinion, they would respond to it. Therefore, every parent should dialogue with their school administrators. Plan a conference with the principal where your children attend. Discuss the following: (a) Education is reflective of a competitive society, therefore, ask your principal to explain standardized tests, numerical grading, and other forms of academic competition. Ask for a comparison of your child's grades with the local school system. Then request a comparison of your child with national norms.

Indicate you will cooperate with the school to see that your child scores above the national norms. (b) Ask your principal to employ only proven educational methodology and techniques. Resist any efforts to make your public school a laboratory for new innovations in education. Judge new innovations by comparing statistical results with national norms. But tests are not enough, ask your principal to judge any new innovation by evaluating the total personality of pupils in the experimental program. (c) Tell your public school administrators that you support higher academic standards. (d) Your principal should know that you favor the traditional academic "core" courses and that your child should not be allowed to sign up for a new semester without parental consultation.

(2) *Attend school functions.* Your presence at school functions may seem inconsequential, yet administrators are often left in the dark to make educational decisions because they do not know parents' desires for the education of children.

(3) *The father of the home should be involved.* Often the mother shows up at the school to make a complaint or work on a committee. The father can talk to the principal as "man to man" if he in fact is male. Usually when the father is involved, the total home supports the public school.

The Classroom Teacher

(1) *Visit the school and sit in your child's class.* Very seldom do parents attend the class of their children, but any school teacher would be happy for the prospect of a close relationship to the home.

(2) *Volunteer as teacher assistant.* Many schools re-

quest mothers to come and assist the school program as: library helpers, supervise the playground, supervise lunchrooms, distribute art supplies, and a thousand other small details that can free a teacher's time for instruction.

(3) *Let the teacher know you will work with your child for improvement.* When the home supports the school, the child usually does better in all of his subjects. Parents can ask teachers what they can do to help the child improve.

Ask the Teacher, "Why?"

(4) *Ask the teacher why your child scores poorly.* Many times parents blame teachers for the low score of their students. As a result, teachers become defensive and cannot work well with parents. When the two can analyze the child's weakness, they can begin to solve his problems.

(5) *Examine the papers the child brings home.* Parents should be interested in all of the papers their child brings home. If he doesn't bring them home, ask for them. If the child's school work still is unavailable, contact the teacher.

(6) *If the classroom teacher does not give you satisfaction, ask for an administrator-teacher-parent conference.* Many parents draw into a shell when they can't get satisfaction from the teacher. They rationalize, "The teacher will grade-down my child if I complain to the principal." However, the child's education is more important than his grade. Discuss frankly the problem with the teacher, but don't let the issue stop there. Come back within two weeks for a conference with the teacher to find what progress has been made on the item.

Mass Media

The mass media has been a primary tool by counter-revolutionaries. A vocal minority has found an issue, then they picket or demonstrate. Because their protest is visible, the television cameras show up. Newspaper reporters seek explosive issues knowing this sells papers. The media are not interested in protecting *status quo*, rather they support an innovative idea . . . novelty, change and uniqueness get the headlines. They only give attention to attacks on the establishment. Our schools are drifting away from the American ethic. The shoe has shifted to the other foot. Permissiveness and lawlessness have become the standard of our institutions. Therefore, we who protest the post-American ethic of our public schools are no longer the protectors of institutions. Now we are the agitators.

Say What You Think

(1) *Communicate your opinion to media.* Write a letter to the editor or phone a commentator on a talk show. When a meeting is held to protest the public schools, make sure reporters and cameramen are invited. When a news event is portrayed on television that irritates you, phone the station to register a complaint.

Lose Your "Cool"

(2) *Lose your cool.* If this book said, "get mad," we would be guilty of stirring up feeling. Those who are running our schools are responsible for stirring up tempers. If public schools make you downright mad . . . show it. By being kind, people have walked over your opinions. By entering into consensus, we have compromised our con-

victions. If somebody raped your daughter, you would be livid with rage. Character rape is going on in our schools. "Start yelling!"

Supportive Institutions

America has a number of supportive institutions, each one has a vital investment in the public schools. Of course, the PTA is the organization most concerned with the schools and *every* parent should be involved.

(1) *Work through the church.* If you are not a Christian, you have no basis for an objective approach to life. Living in a changing world with a pragmatic morality, a person will not know full truth. Accepting God as your creator and the Bible as your authority will give direction to your life. If you obeyed the Word of God, you would become a child of God (Romans 3:23, 6:23, 5:8, 10:9–10, John 1:12). Many Christians have deserted the institutional church for various reasons. The majority of mainline denominations have drifted into liberal theology and their permissive way is no different than the life-style advocated by the public schools. If you are in a liberal church, get out and get into a conservative church. If you have drifted away from the church, immediately get your children under Bible teaching. Then counsel with your pastor concerning the problems of the public school. Let him know your concern.

Tabernacle Baptist Schools in Concord, California, grew out of deep concern by one layman. Your pastor will be a better spokesman to the community than you, but he needs your insight into local school problems. Ask the committee responsible for church curriculum to study the problems of public school education in parent discussion groups. Also, public school officials could be invited to church study groups where the problems of Christians in a secular school could be discussed. Public school educators *need* to hear both the rational complaints and the "gut-level" criticisms against the public schools.

(2) *Work through civic groups.* There are many civic groups who take pride in the community and attempt to enrich the life of the community. Try to get the civic club to which you belong to discuss the failures of the public school. This gives many citizens a platform to air their complaints. Invite public educators to a forum where they can speak about the issues of education and answer criticisms from the public.

Work through other public agencies such as the Department of Recreation, Community Chest, Welfare Agencies, YMCA, YWCA, and other supportive institutions to improve the public schools.

Influence on Legislators

The legislative community is concerned both about the quality of public schools and the opinion of its clientele. Since most legislators give attention to issues that concern a majority of their voters, they will listen to your complaints about the public school.

(1) *Let your legislators know your position.* Tell them you want conservative laws enacted to protect the historical heritage of our country.

(2) *Use petitions.* Legislators will pay attention to a number of voters, therefore if you have a complaint, get a number of other people to sign a petition and send it to your representative either at the state capitol or Washington.

(3) *Ask questions.* If you do not understand what is happening in your schools, write and ask your representa-

tive to explain it to you. Do not make unnecessary work for him, but he needs to know of your concerns.

(4) *Let your legislator know your opinion on the following items:* (1) You should be opposed to the spread of unionism in our public schools. (2) Ask him to revise the compulsory attendance laws for education, allowing parents to determine what is an adequate education for their children. (3) Ask legislators to vote against strikes by public school employees against public schools. (4) Ask him to oppose an absolute tenure system that protects the teacher and saddles the local school with inefficient educators.

Power of the Boycott

A boycott is an effective protest tool. In many cases it is the last resort by those who can get attention no other way. When you take your children out of the public schools and enroll them for private education, this is the ultimate boycott. It is a protest come of age that carries weight at every level of society.

Some citizens boycott the public schools as the first move. They want their children to get a quality education or they want their children to be in a Christian environment. Some boycott the public schools because they are afraid of immediate contamination of their children. These parents don't want to waste time attempting to change the public schools. On the next hand, other parents use the boycott as a final step. They may not have finances for private school. Other parents do not sense the public school is past the "point of no return," therefore, they work long hours to change the public school. Finally, when they find they can't change their schools, they boycott them for the private school.

When we talk about changing one of the largest institutions in America, we are attempting something that is next to impossible. It's like asking, "How can we change the army?" or, "How can we fight city hall?" The public school is the composite thinking of many educators, administrators and legislators. Whereas some public school educators differ in their philosophy, many within the public school system are indoctrinated into its thought processes. For the most part, educators attend seminars and listen to one another. At these seminars they evaluate past programs and make plans for new procedures. Many times they reinforce programs they like and censure programs they dislike. Instead of putting their ear to the sod to listen for the ground swell of society, like the doctor with his stethoscope against his own chest, they listen to themselves.

The Prospect

When preparing this chapter, I interviewed a number of public school principals, asking "How can a parent change the public school?"

"They can't," was their usual reply. Most parents I talked with agreed. Parents who had been to the school had not gotten any satisfaction. One principal of a high school shrugged, "A parent can't change the system, it's like fighting city hall."

"What can they do . . . enroll their kids in a private school?" I ask.

"Parents can't change the public schools, all they can do is work with their teachers to get a better education for their children." His remarks were both prophetic and pessimistic. As I left his office, I resisted asking a final question lest I touch off an argument, "Have the public schools 'had it'?"